Running
Windows
on your **Mac**

by Dwight Silverman

Peachpit Press

Running Windows on Your Mac
By Dwight Silverman

Peachpit Press
1249 Eighth Street
Berkeley, CA 94710
510/524-2178
510/524-2221 (fax)

Find us on the Web at: www.adobepress.com
To report errors, please send a note to errata@peachpit.com
Published by Peachpit Press, a division of Pearson Education
Copyright © 2008 by Dwight Silverman

Project Editor: Cliff Colby
Editor: Jill Marts Lodwig
Production Editor: Rebecca Winter
Copyeditor: Jill Marts Lodwig
Compositor: Jerry Ballew
Indexer: Karin Arrigoni
Cover Design: Peachpit Press
Cover Production: Charlene Will

ISBN 13: 978-0-321-53506-1
ISBN 10: 0-321-53506-5

9 8 7 6 5 4 3 2 1

Printed and bound in the United States of America

To my lovely wife Lisa, whose love, patience, wisdom, kindness—
and willingness to do the dishes while I struggle to make my
deadlines—is beyond phenomenal.

acknowledgments

I've always thought it was a shame that only the author's name goes on the cover of a book. Sure, we who work with verb and noun do the writing, but these things wouldn't get out the door without an army of folks pitching in.

Top of the list to thank is my editor on this project, Jill Marts Lodwig. This may be my second book, but it was the first on which I was the lone writer. Jill's patience and good humor got me through the rough patches. She's also one of the best at editing in a writer's voice. Hey, book authors: You want a great editor? Ask for Jill!

Also many thanks to the great crew at Peachpit, particularly Clifford Colby and Nancy Ruenzel, who helped hone the focus for *Running Windows on Your Mac*, and to Becky Winter and Jerry Ballew, for their production expertise.

I'm also grateful for the help and guidance of my agent, Claudette Moore, and my friend and Windows guru extraordinaire Ed Bott, who introduced me to Claudette.

I'm also appreciative of the patience and support from my colleagues and bosses at the *Houston Chronicle*. I'm particularly grateful to those co-workers who sought my counsel when considering switching to a Mac (and there were a lot of them). Their questions and thought processes gave me valuable insight into what should be included in this book.

Finally, standing credit goes to Larry Magid, whose request for help on *Microsoft Windows Vista: Peachpit Learning Series*, got me into the book-writing biz in the first place.

contents

Making the Switch?

In late 2006, I wandered into an Apple Store in Houston. As is usually the case, it was very crowded, with customers clustering around displays of all the company's products, from iPods to Macintosh computers. I was playing with a MacBook, thinking about whether I might make the switch to a Mac.

To the left of me was a sales associate talking to a couple who were looking with furrowed brows at an iMac.

"So if I want to send e-mail, will this do that? Does it come with Outlook Express?" the man asked. The salesperson suppressed a smirk as she explained that the Mac comes with its own program, called simply Mail. The couple was clearly coming from the Windows world, also considering a switch.

Then, I caught a conversation to my right.

"These new Intel Macs can run Windows now, right?" a woman asked. "I have an older Mac, but I need to run some Windows programs for work. I can do that now, right?"

Whoa, I thought. Two customers using the "W" word in an Apple store! Who'da thunk it? And me, a Windows user, also in here looking to buy a Mac! Three customers lined up at the computer counter, all seriously considering making the switch. Something's going on here!

Indeed. Sales of Macs to Windows users have accelerated. Depending on who's doing the counting and how, Apple's share of the personal computing market was somewhere in the neighborhood of 6 percent to 7.6 percent in late 2007. That's up from around 3 percent in 2004. As further evidence of this trend, the following chart illustrates that the percentage of Macintosh computers accessing a pool of 40,000 Web sites almost doubled from the third quarter of 2006 to the same period in 2007, according to analytics firm Net Applications.

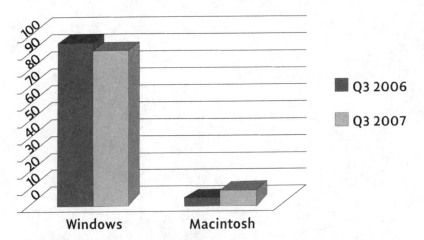

When Two Worlds Collide

Who's buying all those new Macs? During a mid-2007 conference call with investors, Apple executives said that half of all Apple Store computer sales are made to people who have never owned a Mac before.

In my job as a computer columnist at the *Houston Chronicle*, I hear from a lot of readers who want help choosing a new computer. Just five years ago, I very seldom heard from Windows users who were considering a

Macintosh. Today, I hear from several each week. Yes, it's purely anecdotal, but the fact is that most of the Windows users I talk to who are considering a Mac end up buying one.

In the not-too-distant past, the Macintosh and Windows worlds were completely separate planets, and you could not move between them without significant pain. But now that Apple is selling computers that use the same processors that are found in most computers running Windows, the game has changed.

The Macintosh can now run its native operating system, Mac OS X, as well as Windows. In fact, with the right supporting software, it can run almost any operating system designed for Intel and AMD chips. This makes it the most versatile computer you can buy (though that exclusivity stems mainly from the fact that Apple won't license the Mac OS to run on any PC with an Intel or AMD processor). Windows users can now buy a Mac and use its operating system, and still have access to all the software available for Windows.

Good Timing on Apple's Part

Apple's move couldn't have come at a better time. Many Windows users feel as though they under siege by viruses, spyware, and hackers that take advantage of security flaws in Microsoft's operating system. The release of Windows Vista—long-delayed and considered a disappointment by even Microsoft's cheerleaders—also has Windows users pondering alternatives. Fortunately for all of us, the barriers that have long cordoned users into isolated operating-system camps are finally crumbling.

That's why I've written this book, and, most likely, that's why you're reading it. I wanted to write a book that can show you not just how to bridge the gap between the Windows and Mac worlds, but also how to use this bridge to your advantage. Switching to the Mac doesn't mean you have to abandon Windows.

You've got several choices for how you'll run Windows on the Mac. This book covers all of them, and guides you in choosing the method or methods that are best for you. And because you'll be getting to know a different way of computing, this book also provides the basic information you'll need to explore your new operating system.

Most of the books aimed at Windows users who want to begin using a Mac presume the reader wants to kick Windows to the curb; they're full of snide comments about Windows' lameness and the superiority of the Mac.

You're not going to find that here. I understand that you want to use the best tool for the job—sometimes that may be the Mac operating system; other times it may be Windows. No one on these pages is going to snicker at the choices you make. I promise!

What Type of User Are You?

Different types of computer users have different reasons for wanting to run Windows on a Macintosh. They usually can be divided into three general categories.

Windows users switching to or adding a Mac

These are folks who are interested in switching to the Mac, but who still want or need to use Windows. They may have a favorite piece of software they don't want to give up, or for which there is no equivalent in the Mac universe. They may need to use Windows for work that they bring home, or when they are on the road.

There are others who are interested in the Macintosh, but don't want to wander too far outside their comfort zone—at least not right away. Running Windows on the Mac is almost like using training wheels. Eventually, they may want to go all Mac, all the time . . . but not quite yet.

Finally, there are those who appreciate both operating systems for what they are, and want to move seamlessly between the two of them when needed. I fall into this category. For example, I'm writing this introduction on an iMac, but I'm doing so by connecting to my Windows-based PC via software that lets me access it remotely. I am using Word 2007 on Vista because I think it's the best word processor available, and I have access to all my other programs. I'm limited only by the capabilities of the remote Windows-based computer—all while sitting at an Apple computer (**FIGURE i.1**).

In terms of technology, is this a great century, or what?

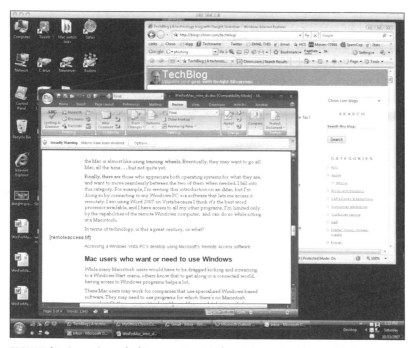

FIGURE i.1 Accessing a desktop running Windows Vista using Microsoft's Remote Access software.

Mac users who want or need to use Windows

While many Macintosh users would have to be dragged kicking and screaming to a Windows Start menu, others know that to get along in a connected world, having access to Windows programs helps a lot.

These Mac users may work for companies that use specialized Windows-based software. They may need to use programs for which there's no Macintosh equivalent. Or they may want to share files and be completely assured of compatibility.

One such user is a friend of mine who works for a NASA contractor that requires each employee to carry a notebook computer—a *Windows-based* notebook computer. When my friend walked into work one day having just bought a MacBook Pro, his boss started to read him the riot act—until he showed him the 17-inch display with a full-screen Windows XP Professional desktop.

When he gets home, my friend reverts back to the Mac, and all's right with his world.

Mac users who want to play Windows games

For years, one of the big strikes against the Mac has been the fact that developers either don't port Windows games to it, or if they do, it takes them forever. Even though Electronic Arts recently promised to port more games more quickly to the Mac, that's only one publisher.

The simple fact is, if you want to play the latest high-end games—and you want to play them now—you're going to want to run Windows on your Mac. Fortunately, both the iMac and the Mac Pro have the muscle needed to run the latest Windows gaming titles, as does the MacBook Pro.

However, you gamers are more demanding—you'll want to run Windows in a way that allows for great 3D graphics and full access to the Mac's processor (**FIGURE i.2**).

FIGURE i.2 When this guy's in your life, you want him looking as good as possible.

How To Use This Book

Running Windows on Your Mac is organized with all three of these previously described users in mind.

The first part of the book provides information for anyone who wants to run Windows on the Mac, while the last three parts focus on specific user types.

Part I, Installing Windows on the Mac, lays out the many choices you have for running Windows on the Macintosh. It then walks you through the processes of installing the software you'll need to run Windows, and then installing Windows itself. You'll learn how you can run Windows in a window on the Mac desktop, run Windows programs as though they are part of the Mac OS, and run Windows as the primary operating system.

Part II, Macintosh for Windows Users, is designed to help Mac newbies cope in their new environs. It walks you through the basic differences between the Mac and Windows operating systems, and how you can make the Mac operating system seem more Windows-like. It also shows you how to get your Mac talking with Windows PCs on your home network. You'll learn how to get started with the software that comes with the Mac, how to download and install new programs, and how to take advantage of the new features in Leopard, the latest version of Mac OS X.

Part III, Windows for Macintosh Users, introduces the vagaries of the Windows operating system to those who are new to it. This part of the book emphasizes how to prevent spyware and viruses—a major issue on the Windows platform, which the Mac has largely eluded to date.

Incidentally, upon hearing that I was working on a book about running Windows on the Mac, one of my readers begged me to describe what a Windows virus attack looks like. He's started running Windows on his Macintosh, and he's scared to death that every popup window generated by Internet Explorer means he's been infected!

Once you're finished reading this book, you should have mastered everything you need to know to switch between the Windows and Mac platforms with ease. Let's get going!

Installing and Running Windows on the Mac

chapter 1

Why Windows on the Mac?

Chances are you know folks who are really into the operating system on their computer. They can explain it to you in loving, but excruciating, detail. You might even take advantage of their expertise when trying to buy a computer. But you're also apt to avoid them at parties!

You, on the other hand, are a bit more pragmatic. You are aware that some programs that are stellar on one operating system may not even be available for another. I am a good example of that type of person. I write a blog, and I love using Microsoft's Windows Live Writer to compose and edit my entries. However, I also love my MacBook, but Microsoft doesn't make a version of Windows Live Writer for the Mac.

Fortunately, I can now run Windows on my MacBook, even at the same time that the Mac operating system is running. This capability represents a sea change in computing. In this chapter, we'll look at how this change came about, and what you'll need to take advantage of this new era.

Apple vs. Microsoft

To understand the benefits of running Windows on a Mac, it helps to know a little bit about the how Apple and Microsoft approach personal computing. The two companies have very different philosophies, but they intersect at enough points that compatibility is no longer the issue it once was.

The Apple Way

From its beginnings as a company, Apple's philosophy has been to develop and sell both the hardware and software for its computers. There have been a few exceptions to this. In the late 1980s, it licensed a few manufacturers to produce their own versions of the Apple II. And from 1995 to 1997, Apple licensed the Mac operating system to a handful of computer makers in an attempt to increase the company's market share. That program ended with Steve Jobs' return to Apple as its chief executive.

Apple's hardware and software are designed to work together. Because Apple controls the engineering of both, the company argues, it can provide a better experience in terms of how easy the computer is to use and its reliability. Apple's control over hardware means there are a limited number of configurations its software must support, resulting in a more stable operating system.

Of course, this also means that Apple controls the pricing and availability of its products. While Apple must compete with PC makers to a certain extent, because it's the only seller of Macintosh computers, it can largely set its own prices for them.

This approach is why you can run Windows on a Mac, but the reverse is not true—you can't run the Mac operating system on a generic PC. There are good business reasons for this. If Apple were to allow any old computer to run the Mac operating system, its developers would have to take into account any hardware on which the operating system might be installed. Its development and technical support costs would skyrocket, and Apple would no longer be able to guarantee a uniform experience on all Macs.

The Microsoft Way

Microsoft is the dominant personal computing platform and got that way by being more than a little, um, *promiscuous*.

Microsoft, you see, will play with anyone, licensing its Windows software to whoever wants to build a PC around it. Giants like Dell, HP, Sony, and Toshiba can make PCs that run Windows. Smaller companies who sell online or in the strip mall down the street can make them. And even you can go to your nearest computer store, pick up the parts for a PC and a copy of Windows, and then roll your own system.

As a result, untold numbers of companies and individuals build PCs. The Windows universe has reached an economy of scale such that parts are inexpensive, making it easy to build extremely affordable computers. That's one reason why you'll see PCs priced much cheaper than Macs. (In addition, Apple doesn't make computers that are as stripped down as cheap PCs—the company simply doesn't sell products in that price category.)

But there's a downside. Because Microsoft plays with anyone who wants to make hardware that works with Windows, the company also must do what it can to ensure Windows works with that hardware. It works with hardware makers to help them make Windows drivers, but it also makes tweaks to Windows in support of those hardware makers. As a result, Windows grows increasingly complex with each new version and, according to critics, more bloated.

Microsoft also bends over backwards to make sure its newer operating systems can work with programs designed for earlier operating systems. That's why you can still run some Windows 3.1 programs on Windows Vista. However, that also adds to the complexity, and raises stability and security issues. Older code within Windows may not have been written with network connectivity in mind, for example, which can create problems with modern, Internet-aware applications that interact with it.

Intel Brings Them Together

OK, we know why you'd want to use Windows on a Mac. And we know how the two companies' philosophies of computing differ. Now let's explore why you can *run* Windows on the Mac.

From its beginnings, Apple's computers used Motorola processors. In the mid-1990s, the company began using chips designed by a consortium comprised of IBM, Apple, and Motorola. Those PowerPC chips, as they were known, carried Apple into the mid-2000s, but they soon began to reach the limits of their architecture. Processors from rival Intel were handily beating the PowerPC chips in terms of speed and energy savings.

When Apple first began selling Intel-based Macs in January 2006, enthusiasts immediately began trying to figure out ways to get Windows to run on the new computers. Since Windows runs on the same Intel chips found in the latest Macs, it seemed an obvious thing to try.

However, there's a key difference between Macs and the computers designed to run Windows, which involves the way the operating system is launched when the computer first boots up. New Macs use a technology called the Extensible Firmware Interface, or EFI, while PCs use the Basic Input/Output System, or BIOS. Consequently, you can't simply run out, buy a copy of Windows Vista or XP, and slap it on an Intel-based Mac.

Simply put, you need a little help to run Windows on a Mac.

Choices for Running Windows

There are two ways to get Windows up and running on your Intel-based Mac. You can install it onto the hard drive and use the Boot Camp feature in Mac OS X 10.5 to launch Windows when the computer starts. Or you can use *virtualization*, in which Windows runs at the same time as the Mac operating system.

Which one you'd choose depends on how you want to use Windows. Using Boot Camp lets Windows have full access to the Mac's powerful hardware. If performance and speed is important to you, and particularly if you want to play Windows games on the Mac, Boot Camp is the better choice.

If you want to be able to move between the Mac and Windows seamlessly—running Windows and Mac programs side by side—then you'll want to consider virtualization.

This section walks you through the prospects of using Boot Camp, Parallels, or VMware Fusion. By the time you are finished reading it, you will have a good sense of which approach is best for you.

Dual-Booting with Boot Camp

Boot Camp, Apple's solution for running Windows on the Mac, lets you choose at startup whether to run Windows or the Mac. A companion program, Boot Camp Assistant, creates a driver disk for Windows Vista or XP and facilitates the installation of Windows (**FIGURE 1.1**).

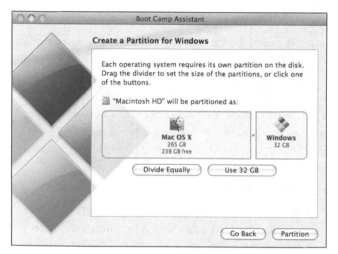

FIGURE 1.1 Boot Camp Assistant makes installing Windows on a Mac easier than installing it on a PC.

Boot Camp is included with Leopard (Mac OS X 10.5) and was originally available as beta program for Tiger (10.4). It is no longer offered for those still using Tiger.

Boot Camp runs Windows natively—just as you'd run it on any other Intel-based computer. Once Windows is installed, you simply hold down the Alt/Option key on the Mac's keyboard to choose which operating system to launch. In fact, if you prefer, you can set up Boot Camp so that Windows is the default operating system. You'll learn more about Boot Camp in Chapter 2.

Virtualization Using Parallels or VMware Fusion

Simply put, virtualization lets you run one operating system on top of another. A program that utilizes virtualization creates a simulated computer, called a virtual machine or VM, which then runs the operating system.

Virtualization lets you run Windows in a window on the Macintosh desktop. You also can run Windows full-screen, so that it looks and behaves as though it's the only operating system active. Virtualization also allows you to run Windows applications without the Windows desktop present, so the programs appear to be native to the Mac.

This book delves into some of the technical details about virtualization in Chapter 3.

The two most popular programs for running Windows via virtualization on the Mac are Parallels Desktop for Mac (www.parallels.com) and VMware's Fusion (www.vmware.com). Both run only on Intel-based Macs, and both cost about $79. Both also require a licensed copy of Windows. They'll also run almost any other operating system designed for Intel-type processors, including Linux and older versions of Windows—even MS-DOS, if you're feeling really retro.

Parallels Desktop for Mac

Parallels was the first virtualization program available for Intel-based Macs, and it was an instant hit when it released in June 2006. Users praised its ease of use and flexibility. Parallels Desktop enables you to do the following:

- Choose from Single Window, Full-Screen, or Coherence mode. The latter allows Windows applications to run directly on the Mac desktop (**FIGURE 1.2**).

- Use USB 2.0 and 1.1 devices.

- Take "snapshots" of the state of your Windows installation and use them to recover from problems.

- Mirror the contents of the Mac's Home folder in the Windows desktop, My Documents, and My Music folders.

- Drag and drop documents and folders between Mac and Windows desktops and folders, and mount the Windows installation's hard drive as a disc on the Mac desktop.

- Synchronize an iPhone to your Windows installation.

- Run a limited selection of 3D games.

FIGURE 1.2 The most common way to use Parallels is in Single Window mode, in which Windows runs in a window on the Mac desktop.

- Suspend a running Windows session, with all applications still open, so that you can open it later without having to reboot Windows.

- Pause a running Windows installation, putting it to sleep without actually shutting down Parallels.

- Run Windows Vista (though not Vista's Aero interface).

- Launch Windows programs when clicking on documents in the Mac, and vice versa, using a feature called SmartSelect.

- Use the Windows installation set up via Apple's Boot Camp as a Parallels virtual machine. (A virtual machine, or VM, is a computer simulated via software. Chapter 3 goes into more detail.)

Parallels also comes with several tools, including Parallels Transporter, which lets you convert an existing Windows installation into a virtual machine; Parallels Explorer, which lets you access the virtual Windows hard disk even if Parallels is not running; and the Parallels Image Tool, which allows you to resize the virtual hard disk.

 TIP

There's a 15-day trial version of Parallels Desktop for Mac at www.parallels.com/en/download/desktop/. However, you'll need to download an activation key by registering with the site. The key is tied to your e-mail address, so if you need to put the trial version on more than one Mac, you'll need multiple e-mail addresses.

VMware Fusion

VMware is a relative newcomer to the Macintosh platform, but it's one of the leading names in virtualization. When it jumped into the Mac arena with VMware Fusion in August 2007, it drew immediate positive reviews. Users liked the fact that its interface better adheres to Apple guidelines for the Mac than does Parallels, and that it makes fewer demands on system resources than Parallels. Its features include:

- Single Window, Full-Screen, or Unity mode, which is the equivalent of Parallels' Coherence mode (**FIGURE 1.3**).

FIGURE 1.3 VMware Fusion, here shown running Windows XP in Single Window mode, has already proven a worthy competitor for Parallels.

- Support for multi-core processors.
- Support for 64-bit operating systems.
- Support for USB 2.0 and 1.1 devices.
- Allows you to take "snapshots" of the state of your Windows operating system.
- Lets you synchronize an iPhone to your Windows installation.

- Allows you to run a limited selection of 3D games.
- Enables you to suspend a running Windows session.
- Supports Windows Vista (though not Vista's Aero interface).
- Lets you drag and drop documents and folders between Mac and Windows desktops and folders.
- Enables easy installation of both Windows Vista and XP.

Now that you understand your choices when it comes to running Windows on the Mac, let's take a look at the hardware and software necessary to get started.

 TIP

VMware Fusion offers a 30-day trial version at **www.vmware.com/ download/fusion/.** However, you'll need to download an activation key by registering with the site. The key is tied to your e-mail address, so if you need to put the trial version on more than one Mac, you'll need multiple e-mail addresses.

Which Is Better: Parallels or VMware Fusion?

Ah, don't you just love competition? Both of these products are excellent, and chances are you'd be happy with whichever one you choose. But there are some minor aspects that may sway you one way or the other.

- **CPU usage.** Earlier versions of Parallels had a reputation for high processor use, which could cause Macs to heat up—an issue that can cause a problem in some notebooks. Version 3 and later of Parallels made great improvements in this area, though Parallels still draws on the CPU a bit more than VMware Fusion, particularly when Windows Vista is the operating system. If you're concerned about overheating and CPU utilization, you may want to go with VMware Fusion.

- **Interface.** The look and feel of Parallels and Fusion are very different. Parallels uses buttons that look like the type you'd see on a media player for starting, pausing, suspending, and otherwise working with the virtual machine. VMware Fusion uses a more traditional Macintosh interface, and it's customizable. Mac traditionalists may want to use VMware Fusion; those who like having quick access to an application's controls may prefer Parallels.

- **Power.** If you'll be using applications that are CPU-intensive, such as video processing, image editing, or CD burning, then VMware Fusion is a better choice. It utilizes both cores in a multiple-core computer, while Parallels does not. VMware Fusion also works with 64-bit versions of Windows, while Parallels does not.

continues on next page

continued from previous page

Which Is Better: Parallels or VMware Fusion?

- **Portability.** VMware Fusion is also a better choice if you want to run your virtual machines on other, non-Macintosh computers. The virtual machines it creates will work in other VMware products, including those designed for Windows and Linux systems. While Parallels' VMs will work with the Windows version of Parallels Desktop, it's not as widely used. VMware has been the virtualization leader in the PC space for a long time.

- **Tweakability.** Parallels comes with a suite of tools that makes administering your virtual machines easier. Parallels Transporter lets you convert a physical Windows installation into a virtual one; Parallels Image Tool helps resize virtual drives; and Parallels Explorer gives you access to the files on a virtual drive even if Parallels isn't running.

- **Vista support.** While neither program will enable Vista's Aero interface, Parallels does a little better job of handling Vista, particularly in its free-floating-applications mode called Coherence. At this writing, VMware is still calling its Unity support for Vista "experimental."

Virtualization vs. Boot Camp

So which of these options is best for you? That largely depends on what you want to do with Windows, and your particular style of working:

- If you want your Windows and Macintosh applications to share files, virtualization is probably your best bet. When you're in Windows via Boot Camp, you don't have access to the Macintosh part of your hard drive. And you can only get to the Windows part of the drive if you've formatted that partition in the older FAT32 file system. If you've used the newer NTFS, you can only read files, but not change them or add any new files to the Windows drive.

- If you're concerned about viruses and malware possibly damaging your Macintosh, virtualization also provides better protection. While most Windows viruses, Trojans, and spyware can't migrate onto the Macintosh part of the drive, some can cause problems, particularly if they try to delete a drive's contents or alter how it boots up.

- If you want to run a 64-bit version of Windows, there's only one choice: VMware Fusion. Parallels does not support 64-bit Windows, and while you can install a 64-bit version of Windows Vista or XP via Boot Camp, there are no drivers for many of the Mac's hardware components.

- If you plan to play Windows games, or run graphically intensive applications—particularly those that use 3D acceleration—Boot Camp is a better choice. Windows runs natively, so it talks directly to the Mac's hardware. It runs faster than virtualization, and all of the Mac's hardware is available to the operating system.

- If you're on a budget, Boot Camp may be a better option for you. Parallels and VMware Fusion each add about $80 to the cost of adding Windows to your system.

What You'll Need

To run Windows via Apple's Boot Camp, you'll need:

- An Intel-based Macintosh with at least 512 MB of RAM, with 1 GB preferred. If you plan to run Windows Vista, consider 2 GB.

- At least 10 GB of free space on your hard drive, 20 GB preferred, and more if you'll be using Vista.

- Mac OS X 10.5 (Leopard).

- A blank CD or DVD on which Boot Camp will write the Windows drivers.

- A copy of Windows XP Professional or Home Service Pack 2, or Windows Vista Home Basic, Home Premium, Business, or Ultimate. This must be the full version, not an upgrade version. And if you're using XP, it must be SP2; you can't install the original version of XP, and then upgrade to SP2.

 TIP

The full, retail version of Windows can be expensive. For example, the full version of Windows Vista Home Premium costs $239.95. But you can buy what's known as an OEM version for a lot less. OEM stands for Original Equipment Manufacturer, and it's the version of Vista installed by people who build PCs. It sells for a lot less, but there's a catch: It comes with no technical support from Microsoft. If you buy this version, you're on your own if you need help. The dramatically lower price may indeed lure you: Newegg.com sells the OEM version of Vista Home Premium for $112 at this writing.

To run either Parallels Desktop for Mac or VMware Fusion, you'll need:

- An Intel-based Mac running either OS X Tiger or Leopard.

- At a minimum, you'll want 1 GB of RAM, but 2 GB is strongly advised. Keep in mind that, using virtualization, you are running two operating systems at the same time. If you'd own a Mac with 1 GB of RAM and only run the Mac operating system, it makes sense to double that amount of memory to run two operating systems concurrently. *Remember, the more memory you can offer a virtual-machine installation, the better.*

- Parallels requires 70 MB of RAM for its own software and 15 GB for the guest operating system.

- VMware Fusion requires 275 MB of RAM for its own software and at least 1 GB for the guest operating system, with 10 GB recommended.

- Windows Vista Business, Ultimate, Enterprise, Home Premium or Home Basic; Windows XP Professional or Home SP2. You can install older versions of XP and update them later. You can also run older versions of Windows, going all the way back to Windows 3.1. You can even run MS-DOS.

Your Options at a Glance

Still undecided about which way you should run Windows on your Macintosh? How about a spiffy chart to all this detail in one place?

Now that you've got everything you need to break through your desktop computing boundaries, let's install Windows on your Mac!

TABLE 1.1 Boot Camp or Virtualization?

Feature or Requirement	Boot Camp	Parallels Desktop for Mac	VMWare Fusion
System requirements	Intel-based Mac; 512 MB of RAM; enough disk space for both Leopard and the Windows operating system that will be used	Intel-based Mac; 512 MB of RAM, 1 GB or more recommended. 70 MB disk space for Parallels Desktop, 15 GB recommended for each Windows virtual machine; Mac OS 10.4 or later.	Intel-based Mac (Core 2 Duo or Xeon processor is required for 64-bit operating systems); 512 MB of RAM, 1 GB or more recommended; 275 MB disk space for VMware Fusion, 1 GB free disk space for each virtual machine, 10 GB or more recommended; Mac OS X 10.4.9 or later
Windows version support	Windows XP Service Pack 2, Windows Vista all versions	All Windows versions back to 3.1, including Windows XP Professional and Home; Windows Vista Business, Ultimate, Enterprise, Home Premium, Home Basic.	All Windows versions back to 3.1, including Windows XP Professional and Home; Windows Vista Business, Ultimate, Enterprise, Home Premium, Home Basic.
Price	Free (with Leopard)	$79	$79
Windows view	Full screen only	Single Window, Full-Screen, Coherence (free-floating apps)	Single Window, Full-Screen, Unity (free-floating apps)
Interface style	Windows	"Tape recorder style" buttons	Adheres to Mac design guidelines
Share files/folders between OSes	Partial (Mac can see Win files, but not vice-versa)	Yes	Yes
Setup assistant	Yes	Yes	Yes
Support for 64-bit Windows	No (installable, but no driver support)	No	Yes (Vista Business/Enterprise/Ultimate; Windows XP Pro; Windows Server 2003
Run Mac, Windows programs side by side	No	Yes	Yes

continues on next page

continued from previous page

TABLE 1.1 Boot Camp or Virtualization?

Feature or Requirement	Boot Camp	Parallels Desktop for Mac	VMWare Fusion
Choose which files launch programs in either OS	No	Yes	No
Treat Boot Camp partition as a virtual machine	N/A	Yes	Yes
Drivers included	Yes	Yes (via Parallels Tools)	Yes (via VMWare Tools)
3D graphics support	Yes	Partial	Partial
Vista Aero interface support	Yes	No	No
Bluetooth support	Yes	Yes	Yes
Wi-Fi support	Yes	Yes (via hardware pass-through)	Yes (via hardware pass-through)
Ethernet support	Yes	Yes (via hardware pass-through)	Yes (via hardware pass-through)
Firewire support	Yes	No	No
USB 2.0 support	Yes	Yes	Yes
iSight support	Yes	Requires Boot Camp driver	Requires Boot Camp driver
Restore previous system state	Yes, using Windows's System Restore	Yes, using snapshot	Yes, using snapshot
Suspend (Hibernate)	Yes (Hibernate)	Yes	Yes
Pause (Sleep)	Yes	Yes	No
Works with Expose	No	Yes	Yes
Utilities	Boot Camp Assistant	Parallels Explorer, Parallels Image Tool, Parallels Transporter	VMWare Converter (optional download)

continues on next page

continued from previous page

TABLE 1.1 Boot Camp or Virtualization?

Feature or Requirement	Boot Camp	Parallels Desktop for Mac	VMWare Fusion
Pros	Fastest Windows performance; 3D graphics support matches actual hardware; simple setup and installation; support for all Macintosh hardware features; support for multiple-core CPUs	Run multiple operating systems at once; drag-and-drop files between OS windows and desktops; choose whether Mac or Windows programs open specific file types; choose how Windows runs (Full-Screen, Single Window, Coherence); run any version of Windows; simple setup and installation; copy virtual machines to other computers; use Boot Camp partition as a virtual machine; better protection from malware; includes utility suite	Run multiple operating systems at once; drag-and-drop files between OS windows and desktops; choose how Windows runs (Full-Screen, Single Window, Coherence); run any version of Windows, including 64-bit versions; supports mutliple-core CPUs; simple setup and installation; copy virtual machines to other computers; use Boot Camp partition as a virtual machine; better protection from malware
Cons	Must reboot to switch operating systems; only runs Windows in full-screen mode; can't access the Mac partition in Windows; can't write to the Windows partition in the Mac OS unless older FAT32 file system is in use; requires Apple to supply driver updates; some Windows malware can damage the Mac partition; no support for 64-bit versions of Windows	Slower performance than running natively; may put a strain on slower CPUs; requires the host machine to have lots of RAM; weak 3D graphics support; no Vista Aero support; no Firewire support; no support for 64-bit versions; no support for multiple-core CPUs	Slower performance than running natively; requires the host machine to have lots of RAM; weak 3D graphics support; no Vista Aero support; no Firewire support; no included utility suite; Windows Vista support in Unity mode is "experimental"

chapter 2

Using Boot Camp

Let a die-hard Mac user watch your Macintosh boot up directly to the Windows desktop and, depending on his or her mindset, the reaction will be horror, grief, outrage or—if you're lucky—curiosity.

But even he'll have to admit—a clean installation of Windows Vista on the iMac's 24-inch monitor is a thing of beauty (at least once all the drivers are installed and the Aero interface is working . . .).

The simplest way to get from the Mac startup sound to the Windows Start menu is by running Windows natively, and that's done via Boot Camp, the new dual-booting feature that's part of Mac OS 10.5 Leopard. It lets you choose at startup whether to launch the Windows or Mac operating system. It's what you'll want to use if you are using any graphically intensive applications and Windows games, or if you'd rather avoid the layer of complexity added by virtualization software.

In this chapter, you'll learn how to create a Windows partition, install Windows, and choose your preferred operating system.

About Dual Booting

Apple's Boot Camp is included with Mac OS 10.5 Leopard, but it was first introduced as beta software for use with the previous version, Mac OS 10.4 Tiger. The Tiger beta expired at the end of 2007, and it's now only available with Leopard.

Boot Camp is what's known as a *boot loader*—it gives you a choice at startup of more than one operating system. Most boot loaders present you with a menu when they launch and wait for you to make a decision. Boot Camp lets you select a default operating system, and that's what launches automatically when you turn on or restart your Macintosh. You have to take action in Boot Camp before you are given this choice.

All computers boot up using the same sequence of events: Software embedded in a chip on the main system board tells the computer to look for an operating system. Once it's found, control is handed off to the operating system, which completes the startup process.

Boot Camp is necessary because Windows-based PCs and Macs start up using different technologies. Windows-based PCs use an older startup scheme known as the Basic Input/Output System, or BIOS. The new Macs use a system called the Extensible Firmware Interface, or EFI. Boot Camp basically simulates BIOS so that Windows behaves as if it's booting from a PC.

Running Windows on a Mac via Boot Camp is . . . well, just like running Windows on any other computer. Installing it is the hardest part, and even that's not very difficult!

There are three steps to the process:

1. Run the Boot Camp Assistant to create a hard drive partition for Windows, and to begin the Windows installation process.

2. Install Windows using a licensed copy of Microsoft Windows Vista or Windows XP Service Pack 2.

3. Install the drivers for Windows from the Leopard installation disk.

Running the Boot Camp Assistant

Boot Camp comes with the Boot Camp Assistant, an application found in Leopard's Utilities folder. This is what you use to begin the process of setting up your Windows installation. Once you've installed it, you likely won't need to use it again, unless you remove the Windows installation.

Getting Ready for Windows

Before you can install Windows, you'll need a place to put it. The Boot Camp Assistant carves out an area known as a *partition* on your hard drive for Windows. It then paves the way for the actual Windows installation.

1. Open the Application folder, and then the Utilities folder, and then double-click the Boot Camp Assistant. The Boot Camp Assistant launches (**FIGURE 2.1**).

2. Click the Print Installation & Startup Guide button, click OK, and then click Print to print the documentation, in case you need it.

3. Click the Continue button. The Create a Partition window opens (**FIGURE 2.2**).

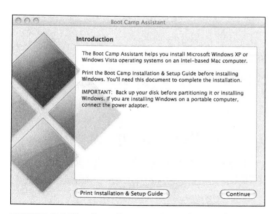

FIGURE 2.1 The Boot Camp Assistant begins the process of installing Windows on your Mac.

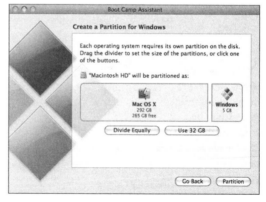

FIGURE 2.2 Boot Camp creates a Windows partition on your Mac's hard drive, letting you control its size.

4. Here's where you decide how much space to give to Windows. By default, the Boot Camp Assistant wants to give Windows 5 GB of space, which is not much. How much space you allow depends on a variety of factors:

    ▪ The version of Windows you're using. I'd recommend a minimum of 10 GB for Windows XP, and a minimum of 15 GB for Windows Vista.

- What applications you'll be installing to work with Windows. Check the system requirements for your favorite programs and factor that into the total you set aside.

- You'll also need to provide space for documents you create in Windows, unless you plan to save them to a secondary drive. If you'll be storing photos, video, music, or other multimedia files, remember that they take up lots of space. Factor accordingly.

- You'll also need to consider how much hard drive space you have available. If you've got a roomy drive, setting aside 60 or 80 GB isn't a big deal. But if you've got a portable or a Mac mini, that could seriously cut into the space needed for Macintosh applications and documents.

Once you choose a size, you can't change it without removing the partition and starting over, so you'll need to choose wisely. Note the Use 32 GB button. Think of that as a secondary default, or as Apple's recommended setting, versus its minimum setting of 5 GB. If you'll be doing the minimum with Windows, 32 GB is a safe choice.

5. Click the Use 32 GB or Divide Equally buttons, or click and hold the divider between the Mac OS X and Windows partitions and drag to set the size you want.

6. Click the Partition button.

NOTE

If you have more than one internal hard drive, Boot Camp Assistant will display all your disks and ask you which you would like to use for Windows. You can then choose the whole disk, or partition a disk with a single hard drive, as I just described.

Once the partition is completed, you'll be prompted to begin the Windows installation process.

Installing Windows Using Boot Camp

Boot Camp Assistant kicks off the Windows installation process, but once it's begun, it's exactly like installing Windows on a standard PC.

Some caveats: You can use any of the four common versions of Windows Vista: Home Basic, Home Premium, Business, or Ultimate. You can also use Windows XP Professional or Home editions, but it must be the Service Pack 2 version. This is important:

You cannot use any version of Windows XP that requires more than one disk. That means you can't install the original version of Windows XP and then try to upgrade it to SP2, either with a CD or downloaded package.

That also means that Windows XP Media Center Edition 2005 won't work, because it is a multi-disk installation.

For the purposes of this book, we'll focus on installing Windows Vista, the most recent version of Microsoft's operating system.

To install Windows:

1. After Boot Camp Assistant has created a partition, you'll see the Start Windows Installation window. Insert your Windows installation disk and click the Start Installation button (**FIGURE 2.3**).

   The computer will restart, and boot up into the Windows installation routine. A window appears that lets you set your language, numeric formats, and keyboard type.

2. Choose your desired settings, and click Next. The Install Windows window appears.

3. Select Install Now. The window for entering a product key appears.

4. Enter your product key and click Next (**FIGURE 2.4**). The license terms window appears.

FIGURE 2.3 When the process is ready, you'll be prompted to insert your Windows installation disc.

FIGURE 2.4 The Windows product key is long and complex—enter it carefully!

5. Select the check box I Accept the License Terms and click Next. The installation type screen appears.

6. Because you are doing a fresh installation of Windows, the Upgrade item is grayed out. Click the Custom (Advanced) item.

The next screen shows you four different drive partitions, giving you some choices for installing Windows (**FIGURE 2.5**). However, there is only one partition that you want to install Windows on, and that's the one named BOOTCAMP.

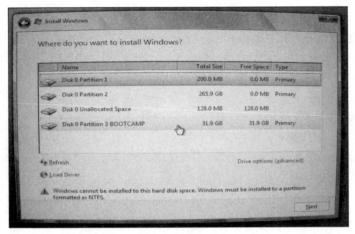

FIGURE 2.5 Be sure to choose the partition labeled BOOTCAMP. If you choose the wrong partition, you may not be able to boot into the Mac operating system.

◆ WARNING
If you choose any other of the partitions, you may lose your Mac OS X partition, and you won't be able to boot into Leopard. You *must* select the Boot Camp partition.

7. Select BOOTCAMP, and then click the Drive Options (Advanced) item. The advanced options appear below the list of available partitions.

8. Make sure the partition named BOOTCAMP is selected, and click the Format option.

9. Click OK in the confirmation dialog that appears. The screen will gray out momentarily, and then return to normal when the process is complete. The BOOTCAMP name will be gone from the newly formatted partition.

10. Click Next. Windows Vista begins its automated installation process.

    Vista's installation is fairly speedy. In most cases, it takes around 20 minutes to do a fresh install of the operating system. Your Mac will reboot once or twice during the process. After the reboots, you'll be presented with a screen that lets you configure your user account.

11. Enter a user name and password, and then choose an image to represent your user account (**FIGURE 2.6**). Click Next.

FIGURE 2.6 Although Windows will let you leave the password field blank, it's a good idea to use one for better security.

12. Choose a name for your computer to distinguish it on a network, and then pick a background. Click Next.

    The next screen urges you to enable Windows to download security and stability updates automatically (**FIGURE 2.7**). The recommend settings also cause Windows to report issues to Microsoft, and will occasionally check for solutions to those problems.

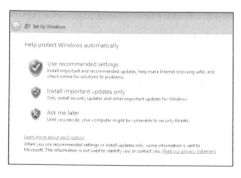

FIGURE 2.7 Using the recommended settings here ensures you get the latest patches and security fixes from Microsoft.

13. For the purposes of this book, select Use Recommended Settings. The next screen allows you to select your time zone and set the date and time.

14. Make your choices, and then click Next. A "Thank you" screen appears.

15. Click the Start button.

    Windows begins a process of checking the performance of your system. Your screen may flash several times. How long this takes depends on the power of your Mac's hardware. When it's completed, you'll be at the Windows login screen.

16. Enter the password you chose earlier and press the Enter key.

Windows will boot to your desktop for the first time.

Now it's time to install the hardware drivers that come with Boot Camp.

Installing Windows Drivers

In the early beta versions of Boot Camp that Apple released for Tiger, you needed to create a CD with Windows drivers on it. But with Leopard, the drivers are included on the Mac installation disk.

To install the driver:

1. Remove the Windows installation disk from your Mac's optical drive and insert the Leopard installation drive. The AutoPlay window appears.

2. Select Run Setup.exe. After a few seconds, a User Account Control prompt appears.

3. Click Continue. The Boot Camp Installer opens (**FIGURE 2.8**).

FIGURE 2.8 The Boot Camp Installer automates the process of installing the latest drivers for your Windows system.

4. Click Next. The License Agreement window appears.

5. Select "I accept the terms in the license agreement," and then click Next.

The next window lets you install the Apple Software Update for Windows application. This application checks for updates to the Apple programs and drivers on your Windows installation.

6. Click Install.

The installer installs the Apple Software Update for Windows and all the drivers. Your Mac may make some musical sounds, which is Vista confirming that drivers for various hardware devices have been installed.

7. When the process is completed, click Finish in the final window.

8. In the dialog box that prompts you to reboot, click Yes. Your computer reboots.

9. When your Mac has rebooted into the Windows login screen, enter your password. This time, the desktop that appears will be in the native resolution for your monitor, and a Boot Camp Help window opens on the screen (**FIGURE 2.9**).

FIGURE 2.9 Explore the Boot Camp Help window to see what the Windows component of Boot Camp can do.

Now that Windows is installed, you'll want to update it with the latest security patches by connecting to the Internet and running Windows Update.

Getting Windows Up to Date

This section presumes you have a high-speed Internet connection, a network connection, or both. You'll need it to install Windows' latest patches and fixes.

To update Windows:

1. Do one of the following:

   ■ If your computer is connected to a network or the Internet via an Ethernet cable, skip to Step 6.

   ■ If you connect wirelessly, on the right side of the Windows taskbar, in the Notification area, right-click the Network icon.

2. In the menu that appears, choose Connect to a Network. A list of Wi-Fi access points appears (**FIGURE 2.10**).

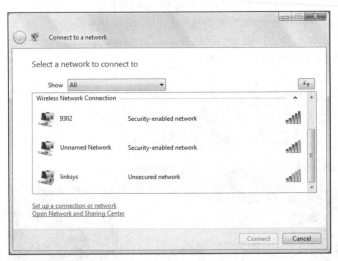

FIGURE 2.10 Windows Vista presents you with a list of available Wi-Fi networks that it has found.

3. Select your access point, and then click Connect.

4. If your Wi-Fi network requires a password or access key, enter it in the dialog box that appears, and then click Connect.

5. In the box that appears notifying you whether your password was successful, leave both Save This Network and Start This Connection Automatically selected if you'll be connecting to this network regularly. Click Close.

   You're now connected to the Internet.

6. You can now do one of two things. You can wait for Windows to recognize you're online, and—presuming you opted to let Windows auto-update—begin downloading updates automatically. Or you can manually start the updating process. To manually update, click the Start button, and then click All Programs in the Start menu.

7. Find Windows Update on the list of programs and select it. The Windows Update window appears, displaying the available updates (**FIGURE 2.11**).

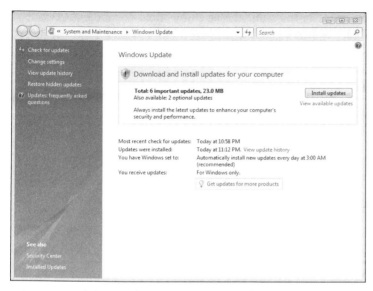

FIGURE 2.11 Windows Update may run automatically, but it's a good idea to run it manually the first time to see what it's downloading.

8. If you don't see any updates listed, make sure you're connected to the Internet and select the Check for Updates item in the left pane. Once you see updates are available, click the Install Updates button. Windows will download and install the updates.

9. When the process is completed, click the Restart Now button to reboot. Windows is now updated.

Now that Windows is installed and ready for you to use, let's look at how to choose which operating system to boot up when you start your Mac.

Choosing an Operating System

By default, the Mac operating system will launch when your Macintosh is turned on or restarts. You can change this if you like, or you can choose an operating system at startup.

Picking an Operating System at Bootup

To pick your operating system when your Mac turns on or is restarted:

1. Restart your computer, or turn it on.

2. When you hear the familiar Mac chime, hold down the Alt/Option key. Keep it pressed until you see a cursor appear on the screen. Two hard drive icons appear. One is labeled Mac, and the other is labeled Windows.

3. Double-click the operating system you'd like to boot into.

   Your preferred operating system will launch.

Setting a Default Operating System

You can choose either Windows or the Mac to start by default.

1. Boot into the Mac operating system.

2. Click the System Preferences icon in the Dock, or choose System Preferences from the Apple menu. The System Preferences menu appears.

3. Click the Startup Disk icon. The Startup Disk properties screen launches (**FIGURE 2.12**).

FIGURE 2.12 From here you can choose which operating system your Mac will use when it boots up.

4. Choose the icon representing the operating system you want your Mac to use as a default. Click the Restart button if you want to immediately go to the other operating system, or simply close the screen if you want to do this later.

You can also set your default operating system from Windows:

1. In the Windows taskbar, in the Notification area, click the Boot Camp icon 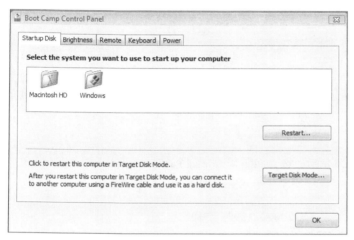 in the Notification area.

2. From the menu that appears, choose Boot Camp Control Panel. The Boot Camp Control Panel launches (**FIGURE 2.13**). Notice that it's very similar to the Startup Disk screen for the Mac operating system.

FIGURE 2.13 You can also choose which operating system to use at boot-up from the Windows side.

3. Select the operating system you want to use as the default and click Restart or OK.

The next time you start your Mac, the operating system you prefer will launch automatically.

Removing a Boot Camp Partition

At some point, you may decide you don't want to have Windows on your Mac anymore, or you may want to reinstall Windows, perhaps with a different partition size. You can completely remove Windows by deleting the partition on which it lives.

To remove a Windows partition:

1. In the Utilities folder, double-click the Boot Camp Assistant.

2. When the Introduction window appears, click Continue. The Select Task screen appears (**FIGURE 2.14**).

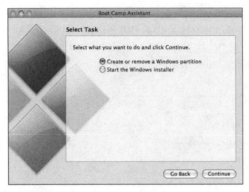

FIGURE 2.14 Boot Camp Assistant can remove as well as create a Windows partition.

3. Select Create or Remove a Windows Partition and click Continue. The Restore Disk screen appears (**FIGURE 2.15**).

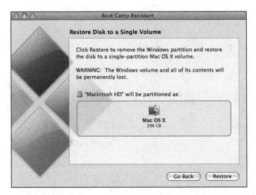

FIGURE 2.15 Boot Camp Assistant shows you how your drive will be set up once the Windows partition is gone.

4. Click Restore and, after a few seconds, the Windows partition disappears.

5. Exit the Boot Camp Assistant from its Finder menu item.

Now that you know how to install and work with Boot Camp, let's explore your other option for running Windows on a Mac: virtualization.

chapter 3

Using Parallels Desktop for Mac

Running Windows on the Macintosh operating system is actually not new. For some time, a variety of products have been able to do this—take Virtual PC, for example, which was originally created by Connectix and later acquired by Microsoft. But most of these programs have been difficult to use and very slow.

The first sign that things were getting easier was the arrival of Parallels Desktop for Mac. It was the first virtualization program designed for use on Intel-based Macs, and it was an instant hit. Mac users who need to run Windows have embraced Parallels Desktop with almost as much devotion as the Mac itself. Parallels is credited today for changing the virtualization landscape and ushering what had been thought of as an arcane technology (a friend of mine likes to call virtualization "the black art") into the mainstream.

In this chapter, I'll show you how to install Parallels Desktop on your Mac, install Windows Vista on your new virtual machine (VM), and finally tweak the VM so that it runs without a hitch.

Understanding Virtualization

Simply put, virtualization involves setting up a software-based computer within the memory of your hardware-based machine. It's a computer within a computer, replete with all the subsystems that are common to a computer—such as a processor, hard drive, graphics adapter, audio card, memory, and display—but all done with software.

You'll recall in Chapter 1 my comments about needing plenty of computing muscle to pull this off, and that's true. When you use virtualization, you're running two operating systems, and you need enough memory and processing power to support both.

Before we go much further, there are a few concepts and terms you should make sure you are familiar with:

- A software-based computer is called a *virtual machine*.
- The physical computer is the *host*, while the virtual machine is the *guest*.
- The operating system on the physical computer is the *host operating system*; the operating system on the virtual machine is the *guest operating system*.

For Windows to run on top of the Mac operating system, you first must install the program that creates the virtual machine, and then install the software for the guest operating system. You can't get by without installing the guest operating system any more than you could get by without having an operating system installed on your physical computer.

Most of the virtual machine runs and exists in memory, but a major component—the virtual hard drive—lives on the host computer's hard drive. (Just as a virtual machine is a computer within a computer, you can think of a VM's hard drive as a drive within a drive.) This virtual hard drive holds the programs and the files that those programs create. Well-written virtualization software, such as Parallels and its competitor, VMWare Fusion, also allow you to move those files onto the host hard drive.

Because a virtual machine is, well, virtual, you can actually change some of its components just by tweaking settings in the software. For example, you can give your virtual machine more memory, increase the size of its hard drive, and decide how its network adapter will access the

Internet. Some programs will even let you use either one or two CPUs if you're working with a physical computer that has a dual-core processor.

Keep in mind, however, that you are still limited by the physical properties of the actual computer. If you have 2 GB of physical RAM, you can't increase the amount of memory in the virtual machine by any more than that, and you must leave some room for the host operating system's programs, too.

When virtualization software works like it should, moving between operating systems is seamless. As this type of software matures, I think we'll see the barriers that have been erected as a result of the different types of operating systems crumble and fall.

Now that you understand the basic concepts behind virtualization, let's put them to use by installing Windows on your Macintosh using Parallels. In Chapter 6, we'll repeat this process using VMWare Fusion.

Installing Parallels Desktop

Parallels Desktop for Mac is available either as retail, boxed software on a CD, or as a download from www.parallels.com. A trial version is available at the Web site. To use it beyond its trial period, you'll need to buy a boxed copy or purchase an activation key. Parallels Desktop for Mac has a list price at this writing of $80.

The installation process involves four steps:

1. Installing the Parallels software
2. Installing the Windows operating system
3. Installing Parallels tools
4. Tweaking the virtual machine's settings

Installing Parallels

Installing Parallels is simple, but you have choices to make during the process:

1. If you downloaded the file from Parallels' Web site, double-click the file to launch the installer.

   or

   If you bought Parallels on disk, insert the disk into your optical drive.

In either case, the Parallels installer folder opens (**FIGURE 3.1**).

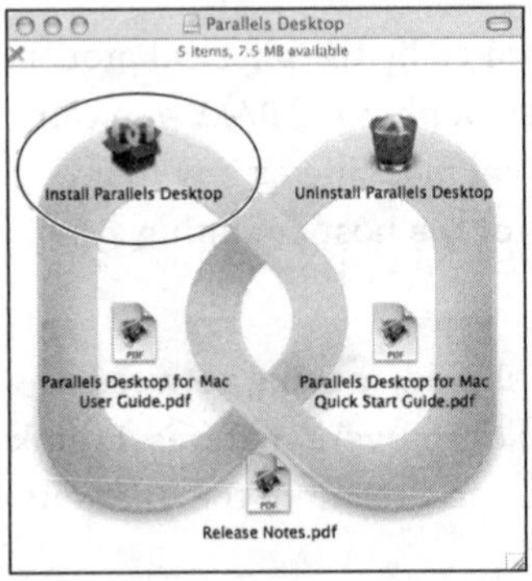

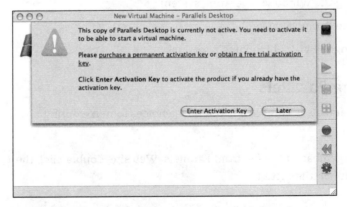

FIGURE 3.1 You can either install or uninstall Parallels from here.

2. Double-click the Install Parallels Desktop icon. The installer launches.

3. Click Continue. The Release Notes and features list display.

4. Click Continue. The license agreement appears.

5. Click Continue, and then click Agree.

6. In the Select a Destination window, click Continue.

7. Click Install. You are prompted to enter your system password.

8. Enter your password, and then click OK. The installation begins. When it's completed, a message window tells you Parallels has been installed.

9. Click Close. The program folder for Parallels Desktop opens.

10. Double-click the Parallels Desktop icon. Parallels launches for the first time, and prompts you to enter your activation key (**FIGURE 3.2**).

FIGURE 3.2 Either a trial or a purchased activation key can be entered here.

11. Click Enter Activation Key, and then enter your Activation Key, your name, and, if applicable, your company name. Click Activate when you're finished. When the activation process is complete, you are asked to register your copy of Parallels.

12. For this exercise, click Remind Me Later or Don't Ask Me This Again. (Clicking Register takes you to the Parallels Web site.) The OS Installation Assistant displays (**FIGURE 3.3**).

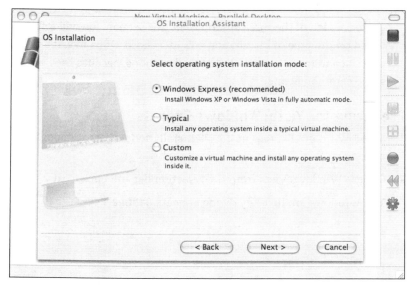

FIGURE 3.3 Here you'll choose what type of Windows installation you want.

13. In the OS Installation Assistant, you must choose from three installation options:

- The **Windows Express** option lets you install either Windows XP or Windows Vista with a minimum of user intervention. This installation is simple, but you'll probably want to tweak your virtual machine's settings when you're finished.

- The **Typical** option is almost identical to Windows Express, with one exception. In Windows Express, you are prompted for your Windows activation key, and you can skip that step when the Windows installer runs. In Typical, you are not asked for a key, and instead Windows prompts for it during its installation. Again, you'll likely want to change some settings once Windows is installed.

- **Custom** gives you more control over each setting, but also requires more work on your part. It steps you through the amount of memory assigned to your virtual machine, the size of the hard disk, and so on. If you choose this option, you likely won't have to return later to tweak your VM's settings.

At this point of the process, the Parallels software is installed. The next phase involves adding Windows Vista.

14. Leave the OS Installation Assistant displayed on your screen and choose which of the three subtopics in this section you will follow, based on the type of installation you just chose. Of course, it's a good idea to read through all three subsections, because they have some common elements.

Preparing for Vista: Windows Express

1. Select Windows Express in the OS Installation Assistant dialog, and click Next.

2. Choose Windows Vista from the selection list and click Next.

The Windows Product Key dialog appears (**FIGURE 3.4**).

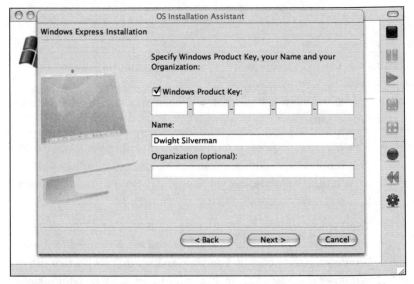

FIGURE 3.4 Enter the product key for the edition of Windows Vista you purchased here.

3. Enter the product key for your Windows operating system, along with your name and organization, if applicable.

4. Click Next. The machine name screen appears (**FIGURE 3.5**). It lets you name your Windows virtual machine and configure settings that allow you to easily share files between your Mac and Windows folders. By default, the virtual machine will use the operating system as its name.

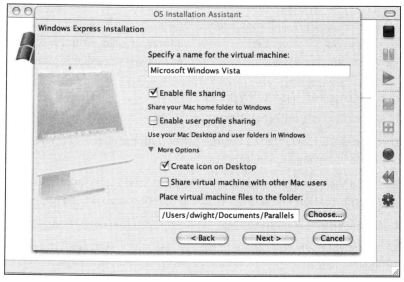

FIGURE 3.5 Give your virtual machine a name, or use the default, which is the operating system name.

5. Configure your installation on the machine name screen. Feel free to change the default name or whatever other settings you desire. Here are a few essentials, however:

   ■ Leave the Enable File Sharing check box selected so that you can access the Mac's home folder from your Windows setup.

   ■ Select the Enable User Profile Sharing option to provide access to the Mac desktop and other user folders in Windows.

   ■ Click the More Options arrow to choose whether to place an icon for the Windows installation on your Mac's desktop, and to give other users of your Mac access to the virtual machine. You can also select a different folder in which to store the virtual machine's files.

6. Click Next to continue. The Optimize for Better Performance screen appears.

7. Select Virtual Machine if you want your Windows installation to get priority access to system resources when it's running. Select Mac OS X Applications if you'd rather that Macintosh programs have priority. Click Next.

   The next screen prompts you to insert your Windows installation disk.

8. Insert the disk into your optical drive and click Finish.

   The Windows installation process begins. Depending on the speed of your Mac, it should take 20 to 30 minutes, and the virtual machine will restart a couple of times. Your Mac, however, will not!

Preparing for Vista: Typical

 NOTE

Keep in mind that you'll need memory for two systems: both the guest operating system and the Mac operating system. There are three things you'll want to consider: How much physical memory your Mac has, how much memory the guest operating system needs to run smoothly, and Parallels' limitations.

1. Select Typical, and click Next. The OS Type window appears.

2. Choose Windows Vista from the list of options; click Next. The name-selection screen appears.

3. Name your virtual machine; click Next. See Step 5 in Windows Express for information about other options. The Optimize screen appears.

4. Select Virtual Machine or Mac OS X Applications; click Next.

5. Insert your Windows install disk into the Mac's optical drive and click Finish.

   The Windows installation process begins.

Preparing for Vista: Custom

1. Select Custom; click Next. The OS Type window appears.

2. Choose Windows Vista from the list of choices; click Next. A memory specification screen appears (**FIGURE 3.6**).

3. Use the slider to determine the amount of memory your virtual machine should use. You may also manually type the amount into the MB field above the slider.

4. Click Next, and a hard-disk options screen appears.

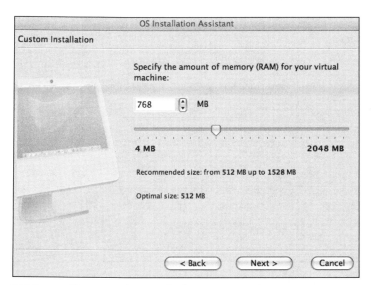

FIGURE 3.6 You can set how much of your computer's memory is used for the virtual machine here.

 NOTE

As I mentioned in Chapter 1, I strongly recommend at least 2 GB of RAM in a Macintosh that will be running Windows via virtualization. And Parallels' virtual machines can only use a maximum of 2 GB of RAM.

5. Choose from four options to set up the virtual hard disk for the guest operating system. For this exercise, I recommend selecting Create a New Hard Disk Image.

   ■ **Create a New Hard Disk Image.** Use this to build a new virtual hard disk from scratch.

   ■ **Use an Existing Hard Disk Image.** Use this if you've already set up a virtual hard disk.

   ■ **Use Boot Camp.** Use this to select a copy of Windows installed via Boot Camp for use in your virtual machine. I'll detail this later in Chapter 5.

   ■ **Do Not Use Any Hard Disk.** Use this option if you want to work with an operating system that boots from the hard drive, such as Ubuntu Linux.

6. Click Next. The hard disk size screen appears (**FIGURE 3.7**).

 NOTE

I recommend setting the memory slider in Step 3 at 1 GB on a Mac with 2 GB of physical memory; at 3 GB of RAM, set the slider at 1.5 GB; and 2 GB for 4 GB. However, I've gotten decent performance from a mere 768 MB in a Vista virtual machine. I would not recommend going below that.

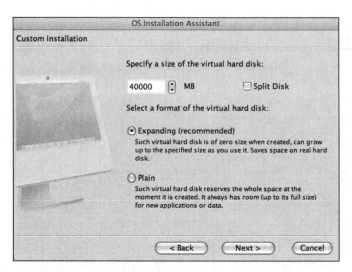

FIGURE 3.7 Set the size of the virtual hard drive based on the operating system requirements and any applications you may install.

7. From here, you can set the size of the virtual hard disk, and do so in a variety of ways. Vista disks have a default configuration of 32,000 MB, or about 32 GB, which should be enough for basic use. However, you should look at the space requirements of the applications you plan to install and change the settings accordingly. You can also customize the virtual drive:

- **Split Disk.** Selecting this option divides the drive into 2-GB partitions. This speeds up disk access, but will also display 16 drives in the Computer folder on Vista if you have a 32-GB virtual disk.

- **Expanding.** This setting allows the virtual disk to only take up the space it needs on your physical hard drive. For example, if you install only Vista, it won't need all 32 GB, and the virtual drive will expand to just the space required. As you add more software and data, the virtual drive expands as needed, up to the total amount you've designated.

- **Plain.** This automatically reserves the total space you've designated for the hard drive from the outset.

For this exercise, choose Expanding and click Next. The networking options screen appears (**FIGURE 3.8**).

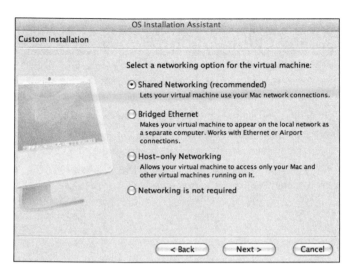

OS Installation Assistant

Custom Installation

Select a networking option for the virtual machine:

⊙ Shared Networking (recommended)
Lets your virtual machine use your Mac network connections.

○ Bridged Ethernet
Makes your virtual machine to appear on the local network as
a separate computer. Works with Ethernet or Airport
connections.

○ Host–only Networking
Allows your virtual machine to access only your Mac and
other virtual machines running on it.

○ Networking is not required

(< Back)   (Next >)   (Cancel)

FIGURE 3.8 Use this screen to determine how your virtual machine
connects to your network.

8. The virtual machine accesses networks and the Internet through
the network adapter on the host computer, but it can do this in a
variety of ways.

- In almost all cases, you'll want to select **Shared Networking**. This
lets you access the Internet and your local network, but the VM is
not seen as a separate system from the host computer.

- Choose **Bridged Ethernet** if you want other computers on a network to see your virtual machine as a separate computer.

- Choose **Host-Only Networking** if you only want the VM to access
your Mac or other VMs running at the same time.

- Choose **Networking Is Not Required** if the guest operating system won't need to access a network or the Internet.

9. Click Next; the virtual machine name screen appears.

10. Name the virtual machine, and see Step 5 under Express Install for
the option details.

11. Click Next, and the optimization screen appears.

12. Select Virtual Machine or Mac OS X Applications; click Next.

13. Insert your Windows install disk into the Mac's optical drive and
click Finish.

Installing Windows XP

Windows XP remains popular with computer users, and in some ways it's a better choice for running a VM on the Mac operating system. It requires less memory and doesn't draw as heavily on the CPU as Windows Vista. While it lacks Vista's advanced features, it may be a good choice for those whose computing needs are basic. If you simply surf the Web, send e-mail, do a little word processing, you can probably get by with Windows XP. For some users, Windows XP may be your only choice—many businesses have their own, custom-written Windows programs that have not been updated to work with Windows Vista. For those folks, XP is a requirement.

To install Windows XP in Parallels:

1. Make sure Windows Express is selected, and click Next.

2. Choose Windows XP from the operating-system selection and click Next. The Windows Product Key dialog appears.

3. Follow Steps 3 through 8 of "Preparing for Vista: Windows Express."

   The Windows installation process begins. Depending on the speed of your Mac, it should take between 20 to 30 minutes, and the virtual machine will restart a couple of times. Your Mac, however, will not!

Installing Windows Vista

Once you've inserted your Vista installation disk, the guest operating system will be installed. It's a fairly straightforward procedure, and should take about 20 to 30 minutes.

After clicking Finish as instructed in the previous session, the virtual machine will restart. If you're doing a Windows Express install in which you've already entered your product key, the Windows installation process will begin without initial intervention. On the other hand, if you chose a Typical or Custom install, you'll need to do some configuring. If you did an Express install, skip to Step 7 next page:

1. An initial screen appears that lets you choose your language, time and currency formats and keyboard method. Make the appropriate selections and click Next. The Install Windows screen appears (**FIGURE 3.9**).

2. Click Install Now; the product key screen appears (**FIGURE 3.10**).

FIGURE 3.9 Click Install Now to get the ball rolling.

FIGURE 3.10 If you did not enter your Windows product key as part of the Express Install process, you'll need to enter it here.

3. Enter your product key and click Next. The license terms screen appears.

4. Check the box next to I Accept the License Terms, and click Next. The installation type screen appears.

5. The Upgrade option is grayed out, because you're doing a fresh installation of Vista. Select the Custom option, and a screen appears for choosing the installation location.

6. The virtual hard drive you created will be highlighted by default. Click Next, and the installation process begins. It should take about 30 minutes.

   When it's completed, the virtual machine will restart, Vista will boot on its own and you'll begin the desktop setup process. The user name and picture screen appears (**FIGURE 3.11**).

7. Choose a user name and enter a password (you can leave that field blank if you prefer not to password-protect your Vista account). Enter a hint if you think you might forget the password. Finally choose a picture to represent your account (you can change this later in the Account module of the Windows Control Panel).

 TIP

Once you click inside the virtual machine's window to make selections, you'll find your mouse cursor is trapped there—you won't be able to move it back onto the Mac desktop. Press the Control and Alt-Option keys simultaneously to set your cursor free. Once Parallel Tools is installed, which you'll do in the next section, this won't be a problem.

8. Click Next; the computer name and background screen appears (**FIGURE 3.12**).

FIGURE 3.11 Pick a user name and a password, which is optional but certainly recommended.

FIGURE 3.12 Enter a computer name, which should be unique to identify it on your network.

9. Enter a name for your computer, which will be used to identify it on a network. Click an image to use as your initial desktop wallpaper. Click Next, and the protection settings screen appears. This screen lets you control how Windows handles updates, checks for problems it encounters and secures the Internet Explorer Web browser.

10. Select the Use Recommended Settings option. The time and date settings screen appears.

11. Click the Time Zone dropdown list to choose your time zone. Vista should have acquired the correct date from your Mac's settings. Click Next, and then click Start at the Thank You screen.

Windows begins a process of checking the performance of your system. Your screen may flash several times. When it's completed, you'll be at the Windows login screen.

12. Enter the password you chose earlier and press the Enter key.

Windows will boot to your desktop for the first time.

When the installation process is complete, the Windows desktop in Parallels appears. It's very important that you install Parallel Tools at this point so that Parallels can run Windows at its smoothest and fastest.

Installing Parallels Tools

For Parallels to run Windows at its smoothest and fastest, you must install a set of files and drivers called Parallels Tools. Without these files and drivers, Windows will run sluggishly, and you'll have to press the Control and Alt-Option keys on the Mac keyboard when you want the mouse cursor to escape from the Parallels window.

When the Windows desktop appears for the first time in Parallels, do the following:

1. Eject the Windows installation disk: In Windows, click the Start button, and then choose Computer. Right-click the icon for the CD or DVD, and in the popup menu that appears, click Eject.

2. Press Control + Alt-Option to bring your cursor out of Parallels Windows.

3. In the Finder bar, choose the Actions menu item and then choose Install Parallels Tools. A warning message appears to ensure the operating system is running.

4. Click OK. The AutoPlay window appears (**FIGURE 3.13**).

5. Select Run PTStart.exe. A message appears warning you not to power off Windows, followed by a message window a few minutes later stating that the Parallels Tools installation is ready.

6. Click OK. The installation begins. You may see several warning messages stating that "Windows can't verify the publisher of this driver software" (**FIGURE 3.14**).

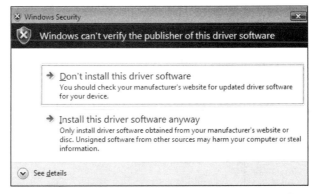

FIGURE 3.13 This AutoPlay window lets you start the Parallels Tools installation.

FIGURE 3.14 Despite the dire appearance of this warning, you'll want to select Install This Driver Anyway.

7. Click the Install This Driver Software Anyway option at each of these prompts. Windows Vista next displays a dialog box asking you to identify what type of network the computer is connected to.

8. Choose Home or Business.

   Once the installation is complete, Windows restarts. When the desktop returns, Parallels conducts an inventory of the programs that are installed for use with Parallels' SmartSelect feature. (You'll read more about SmartSelect in Chapter 4.

Now that Windows is installed, you'll probably want to tweak some settings, particularly if you installed Vista using the Windows Express or Typical methods.

Tweaking the Virtual Machine

The Windows Express and Typical installation selections automate the process of setting up the virtual machine, making some setup choices for you. But in some cases, the defaults are inadequate for comfortably running Windows Vista. In this section, we'll tweak your new Vista installation so that it runs more smoothly.

If you followed the previous set of instructions ("Installing Parallels Tools"), your screen should be displaying the Windows desktop.

1. Shut down Vista. Click the Windows start button, and then place your cursor over the right-pointing arrow at the bottom of the start menu's right pane. A popup menu appears.

2. Select Shut Down. Vista closes, and the virtual machine's configuration screen appears (**FIGURE 3.15**).

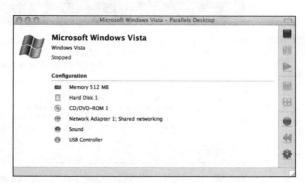

FIGURE 3.15 The Configuration screen acts as the "front page" for your virtual machine.

3. Click Configuration. The Configuration Editor appears (**FIGURE 3.16**).

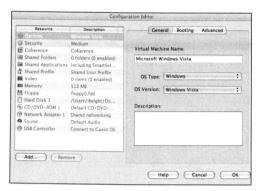

FIGURE 3.16 The Configuration Editor lets you change the virtual machine's many settings.

Note that Memory is set at 512 MB—inadequate for Windows Vista. Click Memory, and the right pane switches to the Memory Options editor (**FIGURE 3.17**).

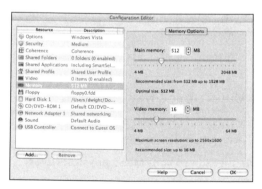

FIGURE 3.17 Use this screen to change memory settings. You won't be able to use more than your physical computer has installed.

4. Move the Main Memory slider to at least 1,024 MB (1 GB) or higher, based on the guidelines suggested in the "Preparing for Vista: Custom" section, earlier in this chapter.

5. If you have a large-screen Mac, such as a 24-inch iMac or 17-inch MacBook Pro, consider moving the Video Memory slider to 32 MB. If you have a large-screen Mac and work with large photos, consider setting the video memory even higher.

   These are the only tweaks I think are required after setting up a Vista virtual machine.

6. Click OK.

The Configuration Editor in Parallels is extremely powerful, and gives you many options for tweaking your virtual machine. Here's a simple breakdown of what each section does.

- **Options.** Lets you change the VM's name and operating system type; the boot device sequence and how the VM starts up; and performance optimization settings.

- **Security.** Controls the integration of the guest and host operating systems. Higher levels isolate the VM from your Mac system.

- **Coherence.** Provides settings for the Parallels feature that allows Windows applications to float freely on the Mac desktop.

- **Shared folders.** Lets you choose which folders are shared between the guest and host operating systems.

- **Shared Applications.** Lets you select whether applications can be shared between the two operating systems.

- **Shared Profile.** If you share profiles, then the two operating systems share key folders. Documents, Pictures, Music, and so on in Vista are matched with the corresponding folders in Mac OS X.

- **Video.** Enables some Direct X features, and lets you set custom screen resolutions.

- **Floppy.** Lets you enable a virtual floppy drive in the VM.

- **Hard Disk.** Lets you disable the hard disk, compact it, switch to a Boot Camp partition or change other disk-related settings.

- **CD/DVD-ROM.** Choose whether to use your Mac's physical CD or DVD drive with the VM.

- **Network Adapter.** Enable the network adapter, choose between shared or bridged networking, change the MAC address, and choose an adapter type.

- **Sound.** Enable or disable audio, and choose from different input and output devices.

- **USB Controller.** Enable sharing of USB connections with the host operating system.

Now that Parallels Desktop for Mac is set up and properly configured with Vista installed, let's start working with your virtual machine.

chapter 4

Running Windows Using Parallels

Because I write a newspaper column that often features reviews of new personal computer systems, those in the market for a machine often ask my advice—and that includes my coworkers. I can always tell when they're seeking counsel, because they usually initiate the conversation with, "People probably ask you this all the time, but ... "

I don't mind doing this. In fact, I enjoy it, because it keeps me in touch with what everyday folks want in personal technology. What I'm hearing more often lately from Windows users is that they are considering buying a Mac, but they also want the option to run Windows on it. Almost all of them, though they are not techies, have heard of Parallels Desktop for Mac, and as Windows users looking to switch, it's an intriguing product for them.

Showing them Parallels in action—particularly running on Leopard— is a compelling experience for Windows users, and usually turns those who were merely curious into bona fide Mac buyers.

Launching Windows in Parallels

There are several ways you can launch Windows in Parallels Desktop for Mac. You can:

- Double-click the icon Microsoft Windows Vista that the installation process left on the Mac desktop.

- Launch Parallels by double-clicking its program icon, which is stored in a subfolder labeled Parallels inside the Applications folder.

- Launch a program installed in Windows, or a Windows component.

- Double-click a document in Mac OS X that's been associated with a Windows application in Parallels.

Yes, you read that last one correctly. You can designate documents on the Mac to always be opened by programs in Windows.

Let's look at each of these methods, and why you'd choose one over the other.

Using the Desktop Icon

This is the simplest, fastest way to start the Windows Vista virtual machine you've created:

1. Locate the icon that Parallels placed on your desktop when you created the Windows Vista virtual machine. It should be labeled Microsoft Windows Vista.pvs (**FIGURE 4.1**).

FIGURE 4.1 Parallels gives you a handy icon that lets you quickly launch your virtual machine.

2. Double-click the icon. Parallels Desktop launches. Vista will start within it automatically.

If you don't mind icons on your desktop, this is the quickest way to get to Windows. Later in this chapter, I'll show you a way to get Windows working even faster.

Using the Parallels Icon

All applications installed on a Mac are placed in the Applications folder. If you're new to the Mac, you can find the Applications folder by double-clicking the hard-drive icon on the Mac desktop. From there:

1. Double-click the Applications folder, and then the Parallels sub-folder. Then double-click the Parallels Desktop icon.

    Parallels launches. If you have only one virtual machine, the program opens directly to Parallels' Configuration screen (**FIGURE 4.2**).

2. Click the green arrow ▶ on the row of controls on the right side of the Parallels window to start the VM. If you have more than one VM, Parallels first displays a list of available VMs (**FIGURE 4.3**).

FIGURE 4.2 From the Parallels Configuration screen, you can run the virtual machine or tweak its settings.

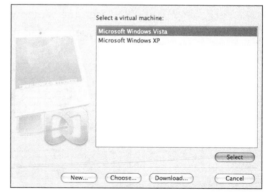

FIGURE 4.3 Got more than one virtual machine? Lucky you! Choose the one to run here.

3. Select the operating system you want to use, and then click the Select button.

4. At the Configuration screen, click the green arrow button mentioned in Step 2 to launch Windows.

Starting a Windows Application

In Parallels Desktop, you can start a Windows program without actually starting Windows first. This is very handy if you frequently use a given program. Since many people want to run Windows on the Mac so that they have access to a favorite Windows software title, this may be the most efficient launch method for many users.

If you'll recall from Chapter 3, part of the setup process involved creating a virtual hard disk on which Windows is then installed. This launch technique involves browsing that virtual disk, finding the program file, and double-clicking it.

1. Double-click the Macintosh HD icon on the desktop, and then double-click Users > Your Home folder (labeled with your account name) > Documents > Parallels.

   In the Parallels folder, you should see the subfolder containing your Windows Vista installation—if you accepted the setup defaults, it should be labeled Microsoft Windows Vista.

2. Double-click this subfolder. You'll see another subfolder called Windows Applications.

3. Open the Windows Applications folder, and you'll see shortcuts to frequently used Windows applications (**FIGURE 4.4**).

FIGURE 4.4 Shortcuts to your most-used Windows programs are found in this folder.

4. Double-click the application you want to run—say, Internet Explorer. A small Starting Microsoft Windows Vista window appears on the desktop. Shortly thereafter, the program you've selected will launch in Parallels' Coherence mode (**FIGURE 4.5**).

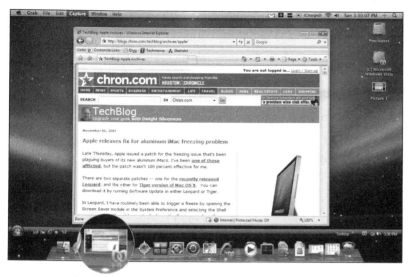

FIGURE 4.5 When you launch an individual Windows application, it runs in Coherence mode on the Mac desktop.

The only sign of the Windows desktop is the taskbar, which appears just above the Dock, and an icon representing the Windows desktop is visible on the Dock.

Note that if you close the application, Windows continues to run in Coherence mode. You have to click the Windows Start button on the taskbar to shut down Windows.

We'll talk more about Coherence mode later in this chapter.

Launching Associated Documents

Parallels Desktop has a nifty feature called SmartSelect, which allows you to choose which applications launch when a document file is clicked, regardless of the operating system you're using. It works in both Windows Vista and XP.

Let's say you have Office 2007 installed on your Windows Vista virtual machine. You can configure SmartSelect so that when you double click a document with a .doc extension—regardless of the operating system in which the document resides—it will always be launched in the Windows version of Microsoft Word. Conversely, if you've got Office for Mac installed, you can have documents on the Windows desktop launch using that suite's version of Word.

 TIP

Don't see the program you want in the Windows Applications folder? You can make it available easily on the Mac desktop. First launch Windows in Parallels and then click the Start button. Next, find the shortcut for the program you want in the Windows Program group, and then drag the shortcut icon to the Mac desktop. Once it's there, you can also drag it to the Dock.

Part of the work of setting it up is done for you. When you first installed Windows Vista using Parallels (see Chapter 3), you may recall seeing SmartSelect conduct a quick inventory of available programs. It's this inventory of applications that lets you pick which operating system will launch a given document.

1. Launch Windows Vista in Parallels.

2. On the Mac menu bar, choose Applications > Edit. A submenu appears with a list of available programs (**FIGURE 4.6**).

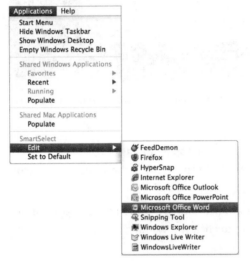

FIGURE 4.6 You can also get to your Windows apps from the Application menu, which appears when Windows is running in Parallels.

3. Select the program whose associations you wish to edit. The SmartSelect edit window appears (**FIGURE 4.7**).

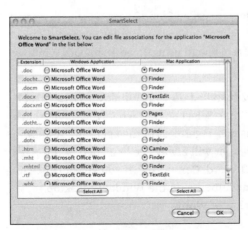

FIGURE 4.7 In the SmartSelect window, document types on the left can be matched with the appropriate application on the right.

4. Match the document type with either a Windows or Macintosh application by first selecting a document type on left, and then selecting the application on the right that you want to use to open it. When you're finished, click OK.

From now on, when you click a file representing that document type, the associated application launches and displays the document, regardless of which operating system you're using.

Now that you know the different ways Parallels and Windows can be launched, let's take a look at the ways you can run it.

The Three Faces of Parallels

As mentioned briefly in Chapter 1, virtual machines in Parallels Desktop for Mac can be run in three ways.

- **Single Window.** In this mode, Windows runs within a window on the Mac desktop. This gives you access to two operating system desktops at the same time, making it particularly easy to drag files between them.

- **Full-Screen.** With this view, Windows fills the entire screen—there are no Mac OS X elements visible anywhere. It appears as though Windows is the only operating system on your Mac.

- **Coherence.** In this mode, Windows applications float freely on the Mac desktop, almost as though they are Macintosh applications. The Windows taskbar is available for managing these programs, sitting just above the Dock.

Each view has its advantages, and you can switch between them quickly and easily. But before we get into the details, let's talk about the Parallels interface.

You'll be able to view and work within the Parallels interface in only two instances: when the Windows operating system is running in Single Window mode, and when you're managing and tweaking your virtual machine when it is *not* running. You won't see this interface in Full-Screen or Coherence mode.

If you launch Parallels in Single Window mode, you'll notice a series of buttons, which Parallels calls the control bar, running down the right side of the window (**FIGURE 4.8**). You'll also see them when Parallels is running, but no virtual machine is active. These buttons control key functions for Parallels.

NOTE

When you launch an application or a document without first starting up Windows, there is a significant delay until the program is up and running. That's because even though the Windows desktop isn't visible, Parallels must still launch Windows completely before the application can run.

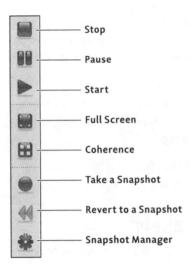

Stop

Pause

Start

Full Screen

Coherence

Take a Snapshot

Revert to a Snapshot

Snapshot Manager

FIGURE 4.8 The Parallels control bar runs down the right side of the Parallels window.

From the top to the bottom, here's what each control bar button does:

- **Stop.** Stops the virtual machine and shuts down Windows.
- **Pause.** Pauses the virtual machine, similar to putting a physical computer to sleep.
- **Start.** Starts the virtual machine.
- **Full-Screen.** Opens the virtual machine so that it completely fills the screen.
- **Coherence.** Puts the VM in Coherence mode, so Windows applications float freely on the Mac desktop.
- **Snapshot.** Takes a snapshot of the virtual machine in its current state. (Snapshots are detailed in Chapter 5.)
- **Revert.** Restores the VM from the most recent snapshot.
- **Snapshot Manager.** Lets you choose from multiple snapshots.

The functions assigned to each of these buttons are also duplicated in the Parallels menu bar items. If you're working in Coherence mode, you'll need menu bar access because the control bar isn't visible in this mode. And if you're working in Full-Screen mode, you'll need to switch to either Coherence mode to access the functions through the menu bar, or to Single Window mode to access the buttons.

Now, let's take a detailed look at the three faces of Parallels.

Single Window Mode

Parallels' default view is to run Windows in a window (**FIGURE 4.9**).

FIGURE 4.9 In Single Window mode, Windows runs in a window on the Mac desktop.

In this mode, you have access to the control bar on the right side of the Parallels window, as well as device icons on the window's bottom right frame. You can right-click or Command-click the device icons to change aspects of the VM's virtual hardware.

Single Window mode also lets you easily move documents between desktops and folders in the two operating systems. If you click and hold on a document in the Parallels window and drag it onto the Mac OS X desktop, a copy will be placed there. You can also go back the other way, from Mac to Windows.

The first time you launch Windows in Parallels, it displays in Single Window mode. If you're in one of the other modes and want to return to the Single Window view, here's what you do:

- In Full-Screen mode: Press Alt-Option + Enter.

- In Coherence mode: From the Parallels menu bar, choose View > Single Window.

Full-Screen Mode

Parallels' Full-Screen view lets you work in Windows as though it is the primary operating system on your Mac. It completely fills the screen, and is best when you're working in multiple Windows applications and don't need access to the Mac operating system.

Entering Full-Screen mode

To enter Full-Screen mode from Single Window mode:

1. Click the Full-Screen button on the right side of the Parallels window.

   or

   From the Parallels menu bar, choose View > Full Screen.

   A message box appears telling you that you can use Alt + Enter to exit Full-Screen mode, or use Control + Alt to release the keyboard and mouse from Windows' control.

2. Click OK to clear the message. You're now in Full-Screen mode.

To enter Full-Screen mode from Coherence mode:

1. From the Parallels menu bar, choose View > Full Screen.

2. At the prompt, click OK.

Giving Windows its very own space

Mac OS X 10.5 Leopard has a new feature called Spaces, which allows you to have more than one desktop. We'll dive more deeply into Spaces in Chapter 10, but I want to use the feature here to give you a feel for the power of running more than one operating system at a time. Combining Parallels in Full-Screen mode with Spaces means you can quickly switch between full-screen views of multiple operating systems.

Why would you want to do this? Imagine working in multiple Microsoft Office windows on one, full-screen Windows desktop, quickly switching over to a copy of Adobe Photoshop CS3 on the Mac, where you're editing a high-res image, and then jumping back to paste that edited image into your Word document. You've got the screen real estate that full-screen views afford and no limitations on the software you can use.

I don't know about you, but I get goose bumps just thinking about it!

To access full-screen desktops for both Windows and Mac OS X via Leopard:

1. Do one of the following:

   ■ If Spaces is not enabled, from the Apple menu in the menu bar, choose System Preferences and then click the Exposé & Spaces icon.

   ■ If Spaces is enabled on your system, skip to Step 4.

2. Click the Spaces selection at the top of the screen. The Spaces dialog appears.

3. Select the Enable Spaces check box, and then close the dialog.

4. Launch Parallels, and once it's running, click the Full-Screen button on the right side of the screen.

   By default, Spaces creates four virtual Mac desktops behind the scenes, each with its own number. You can visualize them as a grid of four, with Desktop 1 and 2 on top, and Desktops 3 and 4 on the bottom. (In fact, as you will see in a moment, Leopard can present your virtual desktops in this view.) If you've followed the steps above, your full-screen Parallels display has been assigned to Desktop 1.

5. If you wanted to get to different Mac desktop, you would press Control + 2, 3, or 4. You'd see a clean Mac desktop with each of those keystrokes.

6. If the Spaces icon ⊞ is on the Dock, click it. Otherwise, open the Applications folder and double-click the icon there. A grid appears showing your desktops (**FIGURE 4.10**). You'll see the full-screen Windows desktop in the upper left quadrant. If any applications were active on the other desktops, you'd seem them as well. Because no applications are running, though, the other quadrants appear empty in this view.

FIGURE 4.10 Spaces shows four virtual desktops, with the full-screen Windows VM running in Desktop 1.

7. Click the image of the Windows desktop to return there.

8. If you wanted to switch back to a Mac desktop, you would hold down Control and press 2, 3, or 4. Or you could click the Spaces icon to return to the grid, and then click any of the blank squares to return to a Mac desktop.

Whoa! This is what Apple's switch to Intel processors was all about!

Coherence Mode

Parallels' Coherence mode allows you to run Mac and Windows programs side-by-side on the Mac desktop. For example, you might have Microsoft Word 2007 running alongside Safari for Mac. You could drag a link or an image from a Web page on Safari and drop it into a document you're crafting in Office 2007. Or, you can go the other way, dragging an image from Internet Explorer 7 into Photoshop on the Mac for editing.

To activate Coherence:

1. In Windowed mode, click the Coherence button on the right side of the Parallels window.

   or

   From the Parallels menu bar, choose View > Coherence.

2. In Full-Screen mode, click Shift + Option + Enter.

The Windows desktop slides away, leaving the taskbar above the Dock (**FIGURE 4.11**). If you have any applications running, they are displayed as free-floating, open applications on the Mac desktop.

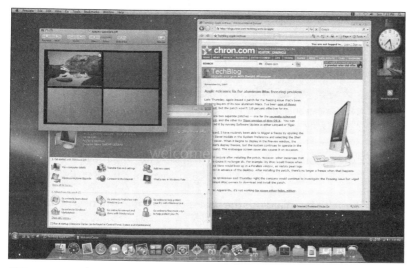

FIGURE 4.11 Coherence runs Windows applications on the Mac desktop, almost as though they were Mac apps.

You can also use these free-floating Windows applications with Spaces enabled. In other words, you can move individual Windows apps onto different virtual Mac desktops, just as you can with different Mac programs. For example, you could put Internet Explorer on one virtual desktop, while Microsoft Word is moved to yet another.

1. In Coherence mode, with at least one open Windows program, launch the Spaces grid by clicking the Spaces icon in the Dock, or double-clicking it in the Applications folder.

2. Drag the image of a running Windows application from one square of the grid to another (**FIGURE 4.12**).

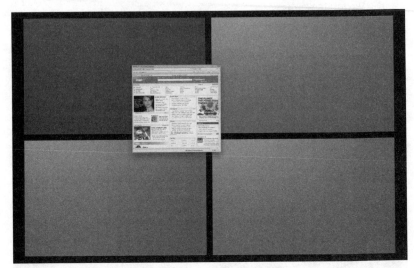

FIGURE 4.12 Moving an application from one desktop to another is as simple as dragging it across the Spaces grid.

3. Click the square representing the desktop into which you just dropped the Windows application. The display switches to that desktop.

Now that you're familiar with the basics of running Windows in Parallels, let's move on to some of Parallels' more advanced features.

chapter 5

Advanced Parallels

What's made Parallels Desktop for Mac so popular among Macintosh owners who also want or need to run Windows on their Mac operating system is its simplicity. As you learned in Chapter 3, installing Windows Vista onto a Mac using Parallels can be easier than installing Windows on a physical PC. And Chapter 4 showed just how easy it is to run Windows on a Mac once it's installed as a Parallels virtual machine.

But there's a lot going on under the hood with Parallels, and in this chapter, we'll explore some of its more advanced capabilities. You'll learn how to back up and manage your virtual disks. And I'll show you how you can use a Boot Camp partition as the Windows installation for a virtual machine in Parallels.

Dealing with System Backups

Aaahh, system backups. All computer users know they should do them, though most of them don't. That's because backing up is often a minor hassle—though it's never as big a hassle as losing all your precious data, *right?*

One of the nice things about working with a virtual machine is that it's very easy to back it up. Rather than having thousands of files to deal with, you've got a handful at most. And when you're running Windows on the Mac via Parallels, you've got several choices for backing up your Windows Vista installation.

Each method has its own benefits:

- There's Time Machine, Leopard's new, super-simple backup feature (which I'll detail in Chapter 11). It backs up your entire computer, and Parallels' virtual machine files along with it, by copying files to an external drive connected to your Mac, or another Mac on your network.

- Vista has its own backup program, the capabilities of which vary depending on the Vista version you're using. It can be used to back up files and folders saved within Vista itself, and I'll provide some basics about how it works in Chapter 13.

- System Restore within Vista backs up the state of your Windows installation within Vista. It's best when you want to revert back after making a system change. Again, I'll explain more in Chapter 13.

- Parallels Desktop for Mac has its own useful features for saving and restoring the state of your Windows installation. One of them is Snapshots, which quickly captures the state of Windows, taking up a minimal amount of space in the process. Another is Undo Disks, which allows you to undo or apply changes made to your virtual hard drive each time you shut down the virtual machine. (Snapshots and Undo Disks cannot be used at the same time. You can choose to use Snapshots or Undo Disks, but not both.) Finally, Cloning makes an exact copy of a virtual machine for use with another copy of Parallels.

In this section, I'm going to focus on Snapshots, which is the simplest, fastest way to easily recover from Windows issues in Parallels. It can even be used to rescue your Windows installation from a virus or spy-ware infection! I'll also cover Undo Disks, which are less versatile, in a sidebar at the close of this section.

Taking Snapshots

The Snapshot feature in Parallels freezes the state of your Windows setup at the moment you take it. It does not copy your entire hard drive, so you don't have to worry about gobbling disk space quickly with many snapshots. There's only one large file—an image grabbed of your system's RAM. How large that file will be depends on how big you've set the virtual machine's memory. A machine with 1 GB of memory will have a 1-GB memory in its snapshot. If you named your virtual machine "Windows Vista," the snapshot files can be found in Documents > Parallels > Windows Vista > Snapshots.

You can use Snapshot regardless of what's happening with your Windows installation. It will work if your virtual machine is paused, or even if it's been suspended. If a program is running in Windows, Snapshot will grab the state of that program, regardless of what the program is doing—so it's best to make sure all disk saves or software installations are complete before taking a snapshot.

You can think of the Snapshot method as a quick-and-dirty backup approach. It's best used just before you make some change to your Windows installation that you are unsure of—installing new software, making a configuration change, or trying something you're not sure will work. Take a snapshot just before you take the risky step, and then revert to the previous state if things go wrong.

To take a Snapshot:

1. With Parallels launched, do one of the following:

    ■ From the menu bar, choose Actions > Create Snapshot.
    or

    ■ On the Parallels toolbar, click the red Snapshot button ● .
    The Snapshot Parameters dialog opens (**FIGURE 5.1**).

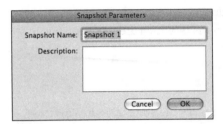

FIGURE 5.1 The Snapshot Parameters dialog lets you name and annotate your snapshot.

2. Enter a name for your snapshot in the Snapshot Name field. If you want to provide more information, such as changes that were made just before or after the snapshot was taken, you can use the Description field.

3. Click OK, and a window appears indicating the snapshot is in progress.

Reverting to a Snapshot

There are two ways to use Snapshot to restore your virtual machine's state. You can return to the most recent snapshot, or you can use the Snapshot Manager to choose a specific snapshot.

To use the most recent snapshot:

1. With Parallels running, do one of the following:

   ■ From the menu bar, choose Actions > Revert to Snapshot.

   or

   ■ On the Parallels toolbar, click the Revert to a Snapshot button ◀◀ . A confirmation dialog appears.

2. Click Yes to proceed. A message window indicates the virtual machine is reverting to the snapshot. When it disappears, your VM is restored to the most recent snapshot.

But what if you don't want to use the newest snapshot? If you have older snapshots, one of them may be a better fix. In this case, you'll want to use Snapshot Manager to choose the appropriate shot.

To revert to a specific snapshot using Snapshot Manager:

1. With Parallels running, do one of the following:

   ■ From the menu bar, choose Actions > Run Snapshot Manager.
   or

   ■ On the Parallels toolbar, click the Snapshot Manager button .

   The Snapshot Manager opens (**FIGURE 5.2**).

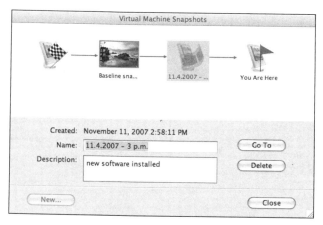

FIGURE 5.2 The Snapshot Manager lets you select, delete, and take snapshots.

2. Click the icon representing the snapshot to you want to use, and then click Go To.

3. In the confirmation dialog that appears, click Yes to proceed.

   A window indicates the reversion is in process. When it's complete, the snapshot has been applied.

Cloning a Virtual Machine

Parallels has a simple feature that lets you copy the files that comprise a virtual machine. Cloning is similar to manually copying the files, though it takes a little longer and is more reliable. You can then take the cloned virtual machine and use it on another copy of Parallels, or store it off your current PC as a backup. Consider using it before making substantive changes to the hard drive, such as increasing its size or

TIP
You can also take snapshots from the Snapshot Manager by clicking the New button. To delete a snapshot, click the icon representing the one you want to remove and click Delete.

running Parallels Compressor (a utility explained later in this chapter). Cloning can be done literally with just a few clicks.

To clone a virtual machine:

1. From the menu bar, choose File > Clone. The introduction screen appears.

2. Click Next. The Prepare to Clone window appears (**FIGURE 5.3**).

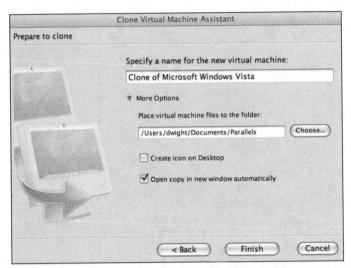

FIGURE 5.3 Click the More Options selection to save your cloned VM in a specific folder.

3. Select More Options to choose a folder other than the default for saving your cloned virtual machine. You can also name the cloned VM here.

4. Click Finish. Depending on the size of your VM's drive and the speed of your Mac, could the cloning process can take a while.

5. When the clone is complete, click Exit. Parallels opens a separate Configuration window.

6. Launch the clone via the Configuration window by clicking the Start button on the control bar if you'd like to test it.

Working with Undo Disks

Parallels has yet another alternative for saving the state of a virtual machine: Undo Disks. This feature works in one of two ways:

- By saving the state of the virtual hard drive in your virtual machine when you shut it down.

- By discarding any changes you've made before shutting down the VM.

The first option is standard operating procedure—when you make a change to your VM, it's permanent, and the next time you launch it, it is configured the way you last left it. However, the second option is more useful. Simply put, it sets Windows to launch with the same configuration each time.

There are several applications for having Undo Disks discard changes. For example, you could use the feature to create a Windows installation just for testing software. You'd set Undo Disks to discard any changes you make, install the software, test it, and then close Windows when you are finished. The next time you launch the virtual machine, your Windows setup will appear as though you never installed the software.

On the other hand, if you set Undo Disks to always accept changes, your Windows installation will behave as it always does, with any changes you've made to the hard disk during a session saved when you shut down Parallels.

Undo Disks does have some drawbacks, though. If you use it, you can't use the Snapshots feature, and snapshots are far more versatile and useful. And it prevents you from being able to compact and compress your virtual hard drives, which can save space. In general, Undo Disks is reserved for specialized and technical scenarios.

To turn on Undo Disks:

1. Launch Parallels and select a virtual machine. The Configuration screen appears.

2. Click Configuration. The Configuration Editor appears.

3. Click the Advanced button on the right to reveal the Undo Disks options (**FIGURE 5.4**).

continues on next page

continued from previous page

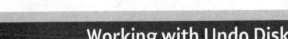

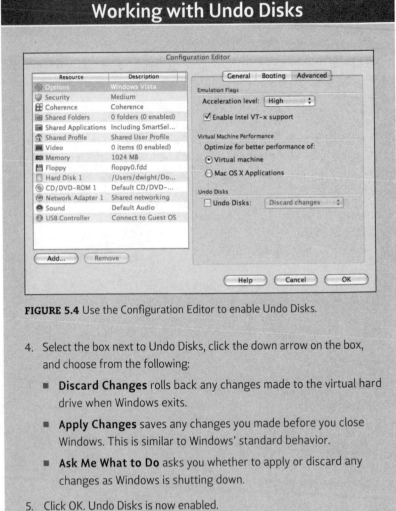

FIGURE 5.4 Use the Configuration Editor to enable Undo Disks.

4. Select the box next to Undo Disks, click the down arrow on the box, and choose from the following:

   - **Discard Changes** rolls back any changes made to the virtual hard drive when Windows exits.

   - **Apply Changes** saves any changes you made before you close Windows. This is similar to Windows' standard behavior.

   - **Ask Me What to Do** asks you whether to apply or discard any changes as Windows is shutting down.

5. Click OK. Undo Disks is now enabled.

Using Parallels with Boot Camp

In Chapter 2, I showed you the simplest and fastest way to get Windows onto your Mac, which is to install it using Apple's Boot Camp utility. Chapter 3 focused on installing Windows using Parallels Desktop for Mac. In many ways, this section brings it all home by showing you how to put the two together—how to use a Boot Camp/Windows installation as the basis for a Parallels virtual machine.

Why might you want to do this? You can run Windows natively by booting directly into it, or you can run it in a virtual machine, all with a single installation of Windows. This gives you the best of both worlds, but you pay for just one Windows license.

For example, if you want to run Windows games, the best way is natively, in Boot Camp (and I'll talk more about Windows gaming in Chapter 15). But using a virtual machine has great benefits, including the fact that you don't have to reboot to get into Windows, and can run Windows on top of the Mac desktop. By using the Boot Camp install of Windows inside Parallels, you have a lot of flexibility.

That said, there are some caveats. You're far more limited as to how you can manage a VM built around a Boot Camp Windows installation because it serves as the core of both a real and virtual Windows setup. You can't suspend a virtual machine that's using the Boot Camp Windows partition, nor can you take snapshots.

Still, for many folks, the benefits, including paying for and installing just one copy of Windows and having the choice to run Windows natively or alongside the Mac outweigh the drawbacks.

To begin, install Windows Vista as indicated in Chapter 2. Parallels also should be installed. Once those two conditions are met:

1. Launch Parallels Desktop. Parallels will recognize there's a Boot Camp partition present and the Configuration screen will appear with the heading My Boot Camp at the top (**FIGURE 5.5**).

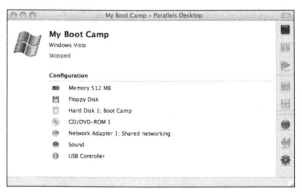

FIGURE 5.5 Parallels is smart. It knows you have Windows installed in Boot Camp and presents the Configuration screen with it preloaded.

2. Click the Memory 512 MB item, and the Memory settings property sheet appears. Remember in "Tweaking the Virtual Machine" in Chapter 3 that I indicated 512 MB is inadequate for running Windows Vista? You'll need to change that memory setting here.

3. Move the memory slider until the Main Memory setting is at 1024 (you can also manually type that number into the setting window).

4. Click OK to close the memory property sheet, and you're back at the Configuration screen.

5. Click the Start button on the Parallels control bar on the right side of the Configuration window to start the virtual machine. You'll be prompted for your administrator password.

6. Enter your password and click OK. The Boot Camp-based virtual machine launches for the first time, and you'll get a warning message (FIGURE 5.6).

FIGURE 5.6 Pay close attention to this warning screen to ensure the Boot Camp-based virtual machine completes its installation.

7. Click OK to clear the warning message. Vista will launch to the desktop very briefly, and then restart.

   The Windows Vista desktop displays, and the Parallel Tools installation launches automatically. You may see several warning messages stating that "Windows can't verify the publisher of this driver software."

8. Click the Install This Driver Software Anyway option at each of these prompts.

   Vista restarts once again, and you'll return to the Windows desktop.

NOTE

You may be prompted to reactivate Windows Vista. Vista will see your use of the virtual machine as a major hardware change in some instances, and want to reactivate. Walk through the Windows process, which usually involves Vista making contact with its activation servers and receiving an all-clear message. At this writing, some users in Parallels' support forums have indicated a few cases in which activation of a Boot Camp partition as a virtual machine doesn't go through. In this case, you'll need to call an 800 number that Vista displays. You'll end up talking to a Microsoft representative who will ask if you are using the copy of Vista on a single PC. Say yes, and you'll be given a new activation key. Enter it, and Vista should then be activated both for Boot Camp and Parallels.

While using a Boot Camp partition in Parallels is useful, there are some things you'll want to keep in mind:

- You can't use Snapshots, Cloning, or Undo Disks with a Boot Camp-based virtual machine, which limits your options for backing up your Windows installation.

- You can't suspend a Boot Camp-based VM, but you can pause one. As indicated in Chapter 3, suspending is similar to hibernating, in which the state of the virtual machine is saved to disk and then shut down.

- Time Machine won't back up a Boot Camp partition.

- The Shared Profiles feature of Parallels, in which document and media folders in Windows and the Mac are mirrored, is disabled. This means you'll need to maintain separate folders for documents in each of the operating systems.

- Any changes you make to the Vista hard drive partition while in Parallels will show up when using Boot Camp, and vice versa. For example, if you create a folder on the desktop while in Parallels, that folder will still be present when you boot directly into Windows via Boot Camp, and vice versa. Any software you install while running in the virtual machine will show up in the Boot Camp side of Windows, and vice versa.

Exploring Parallels' Utilities

Parallels Desktop for Mac comes with several tools that make it easier to manage your virtual machines. In most cases, you won't use these often. But when you do need them, you'll be very glad they are there.

There are three utility programs that come with Parallels Desktop, and one that's built into Parallels:

- **Parallels Transporter** converts physical Windows installations into virtual ones. For example, you can point it at a Boot Camp Windows partition and convert it into a virtual machine. It also will convert virtual machines created in Microsoft's Virtual PC or VMware's products into a Parallels VM. You can find this application in the Parallels folder within the Applications folder.

- **Parallels Explorer** allows you to browse a virtual Windows drive without actually launching Parallels Desktop itself. This is handy when you want to copy a document from the virtual drive onto the Mac desktop, but don't want to wait for Parallels to launch. This is also in Applications > Parallels.

- **Parallels Image Tool** lets you increase the size of a Windows virtual drive for the purpose of adding an additional partition. This can be used as a second drive for storage purposes. The Image Tool can also convert a virtual disk set up as an expanding drive to one that's fixed in size. This is also in Applications > Parallels.

- **Parallels Compressor**, as its name implies, compresses a virtual disk to save space on your hard drive. Parallels Compressor is built into Parallels itself.

Transporter, Explorer, and Image Tool each come with detailed user guides in the Parallels folder. Check those user guides for more details.

chapter 6

Using VMware Fusion

VMware, which has been around since 1998, has been considered the gold standard in desktop and server-based virtualization products. The company is a trusted name in the enterprise computing space. How trusted? Consider this: 100 percent of the businesses in the Fortune 100 hold a VMware license of some kind.

However, until the release of VMware Fusion in 2007, the company had largely ignored the Macintosh market. Its initial version instantly earned critical raves for speed, simplicity, and adherence to Macintosh design standards. It has been winning converts ever since, particularly with the release of VMware Fusion 1.1.

This chapter shows you how to install VMware Fusion, and how to use it to install Windows Vista. It also shows you how to do some initial tweaking so that Fusion runs at its best.

How Fusion Differs from Parallels

Both Parallels Desktop for Mac and VMware Fusion are virtualization programs, which create a computer-within-a-computer to run a different operating system. For a detailed description of virtualization, see "Understanding Virtualization" in Chapter 3.

For the casual user of virtualization, the two programs are functionally very similar (see the feature comparison, "Choices for Running Windows," Chapter 1). However, a few key differences are worth pointing out.

Fusion may be the better choice if you're running processor-intensive applications, because it takes advantage of multi-core CPUs, while Parallels at this writing does not. As a result, Windows running in Fusion seems a little zippier than in Parallels (**FIGURE 6.1**).

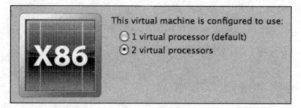

FIGURE 6.1 One processor or two? If your computer supports it, you have a choice.

This comes at a price, of course—expect your Mac to run a little hotter if you're using both cores, and if you're on a portable, your battery will run down faster. Even so, Fusion seems to drag less on the processor in general, demanding less of your Mac's computational resources than Parallels.

In addition, Fusion supports 64-bit versions of Windows, while Parallels at this writing does not.

Fusion's interface is considered more Mac-like and is customizable. It's fairly minimalist out of the box, so you'll probably want to use the customization feature. Otherwise you may find yourself dipping into its menus more often than you need to.

Fusion is a newer product, so it's not quite as mature as Parallels. For example, it does not come with the set of utilities found in Parallels—such as a virtual drive browser, or a tool for resizing virtual drives.

But the competition between the two of them should cause both products to advance quickly. It likely won't be long before VMware Fusion catches up.

Installing VMware Fusion

As does Parallels, VMware Fusion is available both as retail software and as a download from www.vmware.com/products/fusion/. VMware offers a trial version that lasts for 30 days, after which you'll need to buy a copy or enter an activation key. At this writing, VMware Fusion lists for about $80.

Getting up and running on Fusion involves four steps:

1. Installing the Fusion software

2. Installing the Windows operating system

3. Installing VMware Tools

4. Tweaking the virtual machine's settings

Installing Fusion

1. If you downloaded the file from VMware's Web site, double-click the file to launch the installer.

   or

   If you bought the program on disk, insert the disk into your optical drive.

   The installer folder opens (**FIGURE 6.2**).

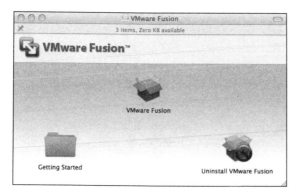

FIGURE 6.2 The installer folder includes ways to install as well as remove VMware Fusion.

2. Double-click the Install VMware Fusion icon. The installer launches and a prompt window displays, telling you that the package contains a program that determines whether the software can be installed.

3. Click Continue. The welcome screen appears.

4. Click Continue. The license agreement appears.

5. Click Continue, and then click Agree. The Standard Install window appears.

6. If you want to change the location of the installation, click the Change Install Location button. Otherwise, click Install.

7. You are prompted to enter your system password. Enter it, and then click OK.

8. The installation begins. When completed, you'll be prompted to enter a serial number (**FIGURE 6.3**).

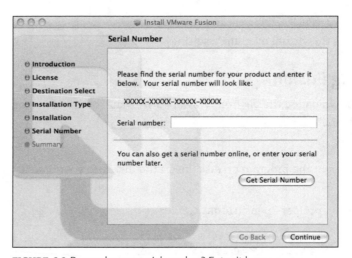

FIGURE 6.3 Do you have a serial number? Enter it here.

Note that if you do not have a serial number, you can still click Continue and use software on a trial basis. You may also obtain a trial serial number from VMware's Web site.

9. Once you have entered your serial number, click Continue. The Install Succeeded window appears. Click Close.

VMware Fusion is installed. Now let's create a virtual machine so that we can install Windows Vista.

Building a Fusion Virtual Machine

Before you can install Windows, you'll need to create a virtual machine in which it will run. The process is a little simpler than in Parallels, but you get less control over how Windows is installed.

1. Open the Applications folder and double-click the VMware Fusion icon. The Virtual Machine Library window appears (**FIGURE 6.4**).

FIGURE 6.4 The Virtual Machine Library is your starting point for creating and working with virtual machines.

2. Click New to begin the VM-building process. The New Virtual Machine Assistant window appears, with the Create New Virtual Machine pane displayed.

3. Click Continue. The Choose Operating System pane appears (**FIGURE 6.5**).

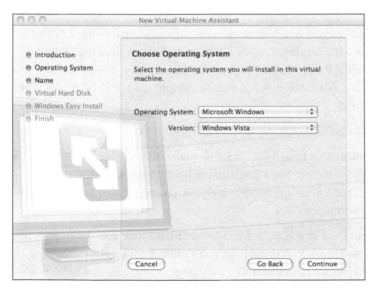

FIGURE 6.5 Choose your operating system type and version here. Fusion supports dozens of different operating systems.

4. From the Version dropdown menu, choose Windows Vista, and then click Continue. The Name and Location pane appears.

5. Name your virtual machine, and if you wish, change the location where the VM will be stored. By default, it's placed in Documents > Virtual Machines in your Home folder. Click Continue. The Virtual Hard Disk pane appears (**FIGURE 6.6**).

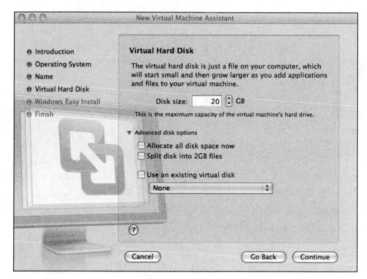

FIGURE 6.6 Use this screen to adjust the size of your virtual hard drive.

6. From here you can determine how large your virtual hard drive will be. As with Parallels Desktop, Fusion by default uses expanding virtual disks that grow as you need the space, up to the maximum you set here. For Vista, I recommend entering at least 32 GB in the Disk Size field.

Selecting any of the advanced disk options gives you some choices:

- **Allocate All Disk Space Now** reserves the full amount of space you set in the Disk Size field, taking up more space on your physical hard drive from the outset, but providing slightly better disk performance.

- **Split Disk into 2GB Files** divides your hard disk into separate, 2-GB files. This option is useful if you're using a file system, such as FAT, which doesn't handle very large disks well. You might need this if you are running your virtual disk from an external drive, which may use FAT.

- **Use an Existing Virtual Disk** is the option you need to select if you have already created a disk you'd like to use. You can select the disk from the menu below this option.

7. Click Continue. The Windows Easy Install pane appears (**FIGURE 6.7**). This screen lets you pre-enter information that Windows will use during its own installation process. The more you enter on this one screen, regardless of the type of Windows installation you plan to do, the less you'll have to do later on multiple screens.

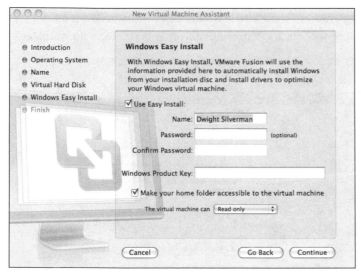

FIGURE 6.7 The Windows Easy Install pane determines just how easy your Windows installation will be. The more you fill in here, the less you have to do later.

8. Do the following:

- Enter your name for use with the Windows activation process and as the account login name. You can also set up a password if you like.

- Enter your Windows product key, and Vista will continue past that screen during its installation process.

- Leave the Use Easy Install option selected unless you plan to do a custom installation of Windows. If you do deselect it, you'll still be asked for this information when Windows itself installs.

- Leave the option Make Your Home Folder Accessible to the Virtual Machine selected if you would like to have the Home folder on your Mac function as a shared folder for Windows. (The Home folder is the folder on your hard drive with your name and an icon of a house. It contains all of your applications, documents, customizations, and so on.) Having the Home folder function as a shared folder gives you a single place to store documents, regardless of which operating system you're using. Then choose whether the Windows system can only read or also write to the folder from the dropdown. I recommend allowing the Windows installation to write to the Home folder—this makes it a little easier to access and work with documents you store on your Mac.

9. Click Continue. The Finish pane appears (**FIGURE 6.8**).

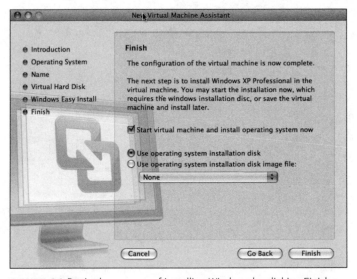

FIGURE 6.8 Begin the process of installing Windows by clicking Finish.

10. Do the following:

- Leave the option Start Virtual Machine and Install Operating System Now selected to have the installation process begin.

- If you plan to use a Vista install disk to install Vista, leave the option Use Operating System Installation Disk selected.

- If you will be using a disk image to install Vista, select the option Use Operating System Installation Disk Image File and choose its location from the dropdown menu.

11. Insert your Windows Vista installation disk, and then click Finish to begin installing Windows Vista.

Installing Windows

The process of installing Windows is incredibly easy in VMware Fusion, particularly if you use Easy Install—there's almost nothing you have to do. Even the process of installing VMware Tools, a set of drivers that improves the way Windows runs, is automated.

For simplicity, this exercise focuses on Easy Install. (If you don't choose Easy Install, you'll spend more time setting up Windows once it is in place.)

Once you've clicked Finish in Step 11 of the previous list, the Windows process starts immediately. Windows loads files, expands, and installs them, and then reboots a couple of times. Presuming that you entered a password at the Easy Install screen, a login screen displays (**FIGURE 6.9**).

> **NOTE**
>
> Unlike the setup process in Parallels Desktop, Fusion doesn't ask how much memory to devote to the virtual machine. The default for Vista is an inadequate 512 MB in Fusion, and you'll want to tweak that once Vista is installed. I'll show you how later in this chapter.

FIGURE 6.9 If you used Easy Install, this will be your first prompt once you've installed Vista.

1. Enter your password and press Enter. Vista prepares your desktop, and the desktop displays briefly. The VMware Tools' setup program launches, the drivers are installed, and your virtual machine restarts. Then the login screen appears.

2. Enter your password and press Enter.

   The Windows desktop displays. That's all there is to it!

I could end here, making this the absolute shortest "Installing Windows" section in any computer book ever written. But because Fusion's installation routine made some installation decisions for you, you may want spend a little time and tweak some of Windows' settings.

For example, Easy Install doesn't let you pick the desktop wallpaper in Windows, which is part of the usual Vista installation routine. To choose your wallpaper:

1. Right-click on the desktop and from the menu that appears, choose Personalize. The Personalize Appearance and Sounds window appears.

2. Select Desktop Background. From here you can pick a different picture or solid color.

You also don't get the chance to determine whether Windows' Automatic Update will fetch Microsoft's latest patches and fixes for you. To get onboard for these updates:

1. Click Start, and then click Control Panel.

2. In the Control Panel, select Check the Computer's Security Status. The Windows Security Center opens (**FIGURE 6.10**).

3. Click Automatic Updating, and the option opens.

4. Click Change Settings. A dialog box appears.

5. Select Install Updates Automatically. When the User Account control prompt appears, click Continue.

6. Close the dialog box. Vista should begin downloading new updates shortly.

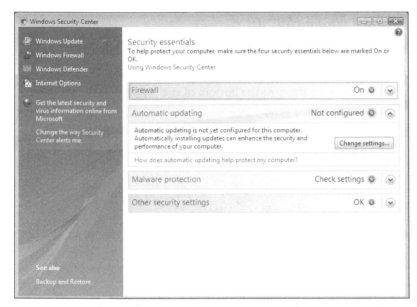

FIGURE 6.10 You'll want to make sure via this control panel that Vista gets updates from Microsoft automatically.

Finally, note that Vista's sidebar didn't launch. If you want to turn that on:

1. Click the Start button.

2. In the search box at the bottom of the start menu, enter *Sidebar*, and press return. The Sidebar appears on the right side of the screen.

Now that you've tweaked Windows a bit, let's tweak the virtual machine itself.

Tweaking the Virtual Machine

Like Parallels Desktop, VMware Fusion makes some decisions about the configuration of the Vista virtual machine, which you need to tweak. For example, it sets default memory at 512 MB, but the versions of Vista that are licensed for use in a virtual environment should have at least 1 GB (see my discussion of virtual machine memory requirements in Chapter 3).

You can change these settings after you've installed Windows.

Adding More Memory

To increase the amount of RAM that your virtual machine uses:

1. Click the Windows start button, and then place your cursor over the right-pointing arrow at the bottom of the start menu's right pane. A popup menu appears.

2. Select Shut Down. Vista shuts down, and the center screen turns black with a huge button in the middle of it. (Clicking the button restarts the virtual machine.)

3. Click the Settings button in the toolbar at the top of the window. The Settings dialog window appears.

4. On the left side of the window, choose Memory (**FIGURE 6.11**).

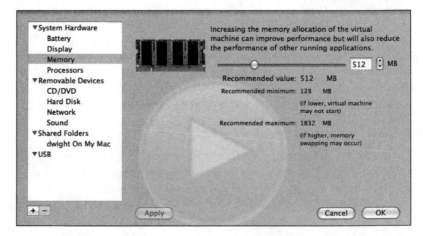

FIGURE 6.11 Use the slider to set the memory for your virtual machine.

5. Drag the slider to the set the memory from the default 512 MB to 1,024 MB. (Note that you may be able to get by on 768 MB, but 1,024 is better.)

6. Click OK. The Settings menu slides away.

Using All Your Processors

If your Mac has a dual-core processor, Fusion can take advantage of it to provide better performance. As indicated earlier, your machine may run hotter and, if it's a portable, your battery won't last as long. But if more performance is important, it's a tweak worth making.

1. With your virtual machine shut down, click the Settings button on the Fusion toolbar.

2. On the left side of the Settings dialog window, choose Processors. The Processors dialog appears (**FIGURE 6.12**).

3. Select 2 Virtual Processors, and then click OK.

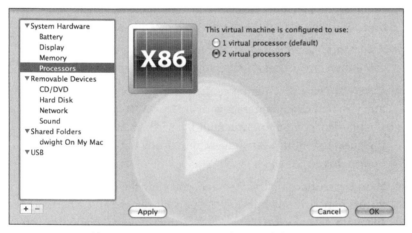

FIGURE 6.12 Double your processing power with just a click.

Expanding Your Network

The default network setting in the virtual machine lets you see the Internet, but not the other computers that may be connected to your home network. To fix that, you'll need to change the way the virtual machine's network adapter is configured.

1. With the virtual machine turned off, click the Settings button on the Fusion toolbar, and on the left side of the Settings dialog window, choose Network. The Network dialog window appears.

2. Select Connect Directly to the Physical Network (Bridged), and then click OK.

Exploring Your Fusion Settings

The Settings window lets you perform all kinds of tweaks to your virtual machine. Here's a quick summary of what each menu item does:

- **Battery.** If you're running Fusion on a notebook computer, checking a box in the Battery dialog passes on the status of the portable's battery to the guest operating system. In Windows, this allows the battery display icon to appear in the notification area.

- **Display.** If you are using Windows XP Service Pack 2, checking a box in this dialog turns on 3D graphics and support for Microsoft's Direct X 9 scheme. At this writing, it does not have any effect in Windows Vista.

- **Memory.** As indicated earlier in this section, choosing Memory lets you adjust the amount of memory allocated to a virtual machine.

- **Processors.** As indicated, choosing Processors lets you designate more than one processor on computers that support it.

- **CD/DVD.** This menu item includes settings for how the guest operating system should interact with a CD or DVD drive connected to the physical computer. By default the settings in this dialog allow the guest operating system to automatically detect and control an optical drive.

- **Hard Disk.** Choosing this item lets you view the configuration of a virtual hard drive. If you click the plus button **+** at the bottom of the Settings dialog on the left, the settings change to allow the creation of additional hard drives for your virtual machine.

- **Network.** As indicated earlier, choosing Network lets you change how the VM connects to a network.

- **Sound.** This option lets you determine whether the virtual machine will use audio input and output.

- **Shared Folders.** Choosing this item lets you enable to disable the sharing of folders between the guest and host operating systems.

- **USB.** This item determines whether USB 2.0 support is enabled and whether USB devices connect automatically to the virtual machine.

TIP

The plus button mentioned in this set of instructions lets you add additional devices when some of the Settings items are selected. For example, when you choose Shared Folder, the plus icon lets you set up additional folders to share between the operating systems. If you have more than one CD or DVD drive attached to the physical computer, you can use this to add it. As you'd expect, the companion minus button lets you remove devices.

Installing Windows XP in Fusion

Unlike Parallels, installing Windows XP in VMware Fusion is almost identical to the process used for Windows Vista. The Windows Easy Install feature lets you input the XP product key and passes it along to the Windows installation process. There is one slight difference, however.

With Windows XP, you have the opportunity to make changes to the virtual machine's configuration that are not available during the Vista setup.

In "Building a Fusion Virtual Machine" earlier in this chapter, after you click Finish in Step 11, the Settings dialog window displays, which lets you tweak your VM's settings before the Windows installation begins. Once you click OK after making any changes, the process continues just as it did with Windows Vista.

The default settings for XP are adequate for memory (512 MB) but possibly inadequate for disk space (20 GB). I recommend 30 GB for an XP virtual drive.

Your Windows Vista virtual machine is now ready to use. Now let's see what it can do!

chapter 7

Running Windows with Fusion

Although VMware has long been a leader in enterprise-level virtualization programs, it's not a household name when it comes to consumer products. And for the most part, the Mac is not a fixture in most businesses—Apple's biggest gains have been in the consumer space. With Fusion, VMware needed to have a product that would be powerful enough to be used at the office, but friendly enough for use in the home as well.

As you probably suspect from reading Chapter 6, VMware has largely succeeded—the ease with which Windows Vista can be installed is evidence enough. But as you're about to see, from its interface to its feature set, Fusion hits a nice balance between power and simplicity, making it a great choice for consumers or business users who want to run Windows on the Mac.

Launching Windows in Fusion

There are two ways to start Windows in VMware Fusion:

- Launch Fusion by double-clicking its program icon in the Applications folder. This launches the Virtual Machine Library, which lets you choose a VM to run.

- Launch a specific VM by navigating directly to its icon. VMs are stored in Home > Documents > Virtual Machines.

Let's look at the differences between these two approaches, and why you'd choose one over the other.

Using Fusion's Icon

There may be times when you want to get Fusion up and running before you start Windows. Perhaps you want to select from different operating system installations, or you may want to tweak some settings before you launch. In these cases, start Fusion first this way:

1. In the Applications folder on your Mac, double-click the VMware Fusion icon. The Virtual Machine Library launches, showing the VMs available to you (**FIGURE 7.1**).

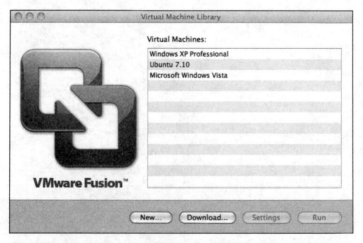

FIGURE 7.1 By opening Fusion first, you can make some choices before launching Windows.

2. Select the VM you want to run.

3. Click Run. The operating system launches.

4. If you want to change settings, click the Settings button instead. Note that most settings in your VM can't be changed if the guest operating system is running.

Using the Virtual Machine Icon

The fastest way to launch Windows in Fusion is to go directly to the virtual machine itself and double-click it. You'll bypass the Virtual Machine Library this way, so you can get right down to business.

1. Navigate to Home > Documents and open the subfolder labeled Virtual Machines.

2. Double-click the icon for the VM you want to launch (**FIGURE 7.2**).

   The operating system you've selected will launch without first going to the library.

FIGURE 7.2 Want to get from Point A to B fast? Double-click the icon for the guest operating system you want to launch.

Now that you've got your guest operating system running, let's look at the different ways Fusion lets you use it.

The Three Faces of Fusion

Like Parallels, Fusion has three modes in which Windows can be run.

- **Single Window.** In this mode, Windows runs within a window on the Mac desktop. This gives you access to two operating-system desktops at the same time, making it particularly easy to drag files between them.

- **Full-Screen.** With this view, Windows fills the entire screen. Most of the time, there are no Mac OS X elements visible anywhere. It appears as though Windows is the only operating system on your Mac.

- **Unity.** In this mode, Windows applications float freely on the Mac desktop, almost as though they are Macintosh applications. By default, the Windows taskbar is not even visible, though you can turn it on as an option.

Each view mode has its advantages. But before we explore them, let me first give you a quick tour of Fusion's toolbar (**FIGURE 7.3**):

- **Suspend.** Lets you save your guest operating setting in its current state. When you use Suspend to close the VM, it will freeze your session in place, including any open applications. When you restart the VM after using Suspend, it opens with the guest operating system running as you left it. This is similar to Hibernate in Windows on a physical PC.

- **Take Snapshot.** Takes a snapshot of the virtual machine in its current state. (Snapshots are detailed in Chapter 8.)

- **Revert to Snapshot.** Restores the VM from the most recent snapshot.

- **Settings.** Gives you access to the VM's configuration, including Memory, Display, Networking, and more.

- **Unity.** Runs Windows applications in free-floating mode, so that they are running without the Windows desktop. This is the same as Coherence mode in Parallels.

- **Full-Screen.** Runs Windows so that it fills the screen, making it appear as though it's the only operating system that is running.

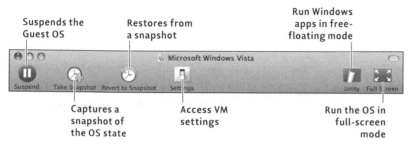

FIGURE 7.3 Fusion's toolbar gives you control over most of its functions.

Each of these functions is duplicated in menu bar items.

Unlike Parallels' Control bar, you can customize the Fusion toolbar.
To change which icons appear:

1. Right-click or Control-click the toolbar, and choose Customize
Toolbar from the menu that appears. A dialog box appears (**FIGURE 7.4**).

FIGURE 7.4 You can customize Fusion's toolbar to your liking.

2. Drag the icons representing features you use most often from the
dialog onto the toolbar. To return to the default set of icons, drag
the entire default set to the toolbar.

3. Click Done.

Now, let's take a detailed look at the three faces of Fusion.

Single Window Mode

VMware Fusion's default view is to run Windows in a window (**FIGURE 7.5**).

In this mode, you have access to the toolbar across the top of the Fusion window, as well as device icons on the window's bottom right frame. You can right-click or Control-click the device icons to change aspects of the VM's virtual hardware.

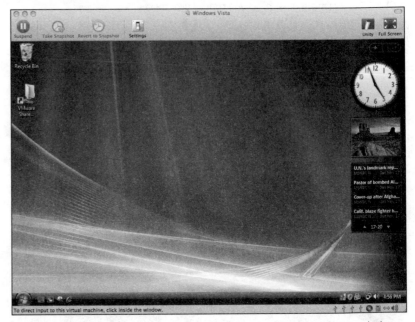

FIGURE 7.5 When it first starts, Fusion runs Windows in a window on the Mac desktop.

It also lets you easily move documents between desktops and folders in the two operating systems. If you click and hold on a document in the Fusion window and drag it onto the Mac OS X desktop, a copy will be placed there. You can also go back the other way, from Mac to Windows.

The first time you launch Windows in Fusion, it opens in Single Window mode. If you're in one of the other modes and want to return to Single Window view, here's what you do:

- In Full-Screen mode: Press Control + Command + S. You can also move your cursor to the top of the screen to reveal the Fusion menu bar, and then choose View > Single Window.

- In Coherence mode: From the Fusion menu bar, choose View > Single Window, or press Shift + Command + Enter.

Full-Screen Mode

Fusion's Full-Screen view lets you work in Windows as though it is the primary operating system on your Mac. It completely fills the screen, and is a good choice for when you're working in multiple Windows applications and you don't need access to the Mac.

It also works well with Spaces, the new virtual desktop manager that comes with Leopard (we briefly discussed it in Chapter 4). But more about that in a moment.

To enter Full-Screen mode from Single Window mode:

- Click the Full-Screen button on the toolbar.

  or

- From the Fusion menu bar, choose View > Full-Screen.

  The Fusion window fades away, there's a pause, and the Windows desktop takes over your entire screen. A small window appears telling you how to exit Full-Screen (press Control + Command + S).

To enter Full-Screen mode from Unity mode:

- From the Fusion menu bar, choose View > Full-Screen, or press Control + Command + Enter.

You can also use Spaces, Mac's virtual desktop manager, to give you access to full-screen modes for both Windows and the Mac operating systems, and switch between them with a simple keystroke.

To access full-screen desktops for both Windows and Mac OS X Leopard:

1. Do one of the following:

   - If Spaces is not enabled, from the Apple menu in the menu bar, choose System Preferences and then click the Exposé & Spaces icon.

   - If Spaces is enabled on your system, skip to Step 4.

2. Click the Spaces selection at the top of the screen. The Spaces dialog appears.

3. Select the Enable Spaces check box, and then close the dialog.

4. Launch a Fusion VM, and once it's running, click the Full-Screen button.

   By default, Spaces creates four virtual desktops, each with its own number. One and two are on top; three and four are on the bottom. Your full-screen Fusion display should be in Desktop 1. To get to any of the other desktops, press Control + 2, 3, or 4. (You won't see the grid of the four virtual desktops unless you click the Spaces icon to reveal it.)

5. Go ahead and press Control + 2, 3, or 4. When you do, your display returns to a Mac desktop.

6. If the Spaces icon is on the Dock, click it. Otherwise, open the Applications folder and double-click the icon there. A grid appears showing your desktops (**FIGURE 7.6**).

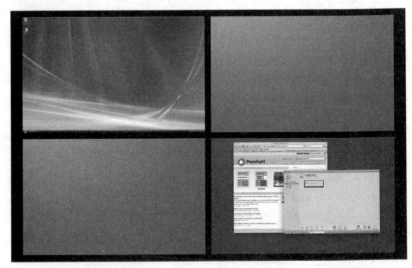

FIGURE 7.6 Fusion running Vista in Full-Screen mode is in the upper-left quadrant in Spaces (Desktop 1); the active Mac desktop is in the lower-right (Desktop 2).

7. Click the image of the Windows desktop to return there.

8. To switch back to a Mac desktop, hold down Control and press 2, 3, or 4.

Unity Mode

Fusion's Unity mode allows you to run Mac and Windows programs side-by-side on the Mac desktop. For example, you might have Microsoft Word 2007 running alongside Safari for Mac. You could drag a link or an image from a Web page on Safari and drop it into a document you're crafting in Office 2007. Or, you can go the other way, dragging an image from Internet Explorer 7 into Photoshop on the Mac for editing.

To activate Unity mode from Single Window mode:

- Click the Unity button on the Fusion toolbar.

  or

- From the Fusion menu bar, choose View > Unity.

To activate Unity mode from Full-Screen mode:

- Press Control + Command + U.

  The Windows desktop fades away. If you have any applications running, they will appear free-floating on the Mac desktop (**FIGURE 7.7**).

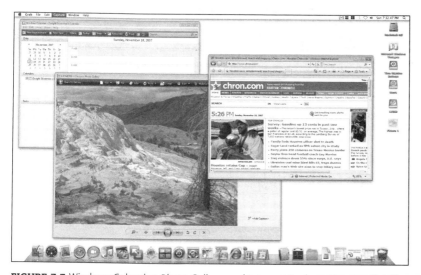

FIGURE 7.7 Windows Calendar, Photo Gallery, and Internet Explorer 7 run on the Mac desktop in Unity, almost as if they belong there!

You can use these free-floating Windows applications with Spaces, moving them between virtual desktops.

1. In Unity mode, with at least one open Windows program, launch the Spaces grid.

2. Drag the image of a running Windows application from one square of the grid to another (**FIGURE 7.8**).

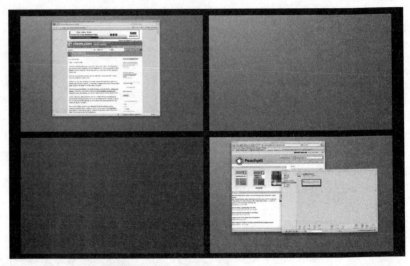

FIGURE 7.8 With Windows applications floating on their own in Unity, you can drag them into any Spaces desktop.

3. Click the square representing the desktop into which you just dropped the Windows application. The display switches to that desktop.

We'll deal with Spaces in more detail in Chapter 10.

Now that you're familiar with the basics of running Windows in Fusion, let's look at some of Fusion's more advanced features.

chapter 8

Advanced VMware Fusion

As is the case with Parallels Desktop for Mac, "advanced" is a relative term in regard to VMware Fusion, and maybe even more so. While Parallels offers multiple ways to back up a virtual machine or save its current state, Fusion offers only one. Where Parallels comes with several handy utilities, one additional utility is available for Fusion as of this writing, and it doesn't come with the software—it's an additional download.

Fusion is designed to be simple and very easy to use, so bells and whistles are not a defining characteristic of this product. Its advanced capabilities are further limited by the fact that it's relatively new. Any additional features in future versions will likely give it more complexity as Fusion matures.

Taking and Using Snapshots

Unlike Parallels Desktop, VMware Fusion allows you to save only one snapshot at a time, which is a way to save the current state of your virtual machine as a quick-and-dirty backup. The snapshot you take will be what you can restore from, and each new snapshot overwrites the previous one.

Taking a Snapshot

To capture a snapshot of your VM:

1. Launch the VMware Fusion virtual machine you'd like to snapshot.

2. Click the Take Snapshot button on the VMware Fusion toolbar. If you have previously taken a snapshot, a warning message appears (**FIGURE 8.1**). Click Yes to continue the snapshot.

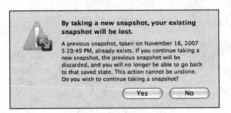

FIGURE 8.1 When you take a snapshot in VMware Fusion, it will overwrite the previous snapshot.

A progress bar appears, and when the snapshot is complete, another progress notice appears, indicating that older files are being deleted. When this closes, the snapshot has been completed.

Reverting to a Snapshot

To revert back to the state saved by the most recent snapshot:

1. Click the Revert to a Snapshot icon on the VMware Fusion toolbar. A warning message appears, letting you know that the state of the virtual machine is about to revert the state saved when the last snapshot was made (**FIGURE 8.2**).

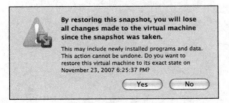

FIGURE 8.2 Reverting to a snapshot undoes any changes made in the virtual machine, including documents you may have saved to the drive.

2. Click Yes to continue. The VMware Fusion window goes black, and the large start button appears briefly, as though the virtual machine has been suspended. The button clears, a progress bar indicates the VM is being reverted, and the desktop reappears. The reversion is complete.

Discarding a Snapshot

You can delete your snapshot to save disk space. Deleting it won't affect a reversion you've already executed. It only removes the files you used to do the reversion.

To discard a snapshot:

1. From the Fusion menu bar, choose Virtual Machine > Discard Snapshot. A warning message appears, indicating that you'll not be able to return to the previous state.

2. Click Yes to continue. A progress bar appears. When the bar disappears, the process is complete.

 NOTE

Any changes you have made to any file in the virtual machine will be undone, back to the date of the snapshot. That includes any documents you may have changed and stored on the virtual disk. Documents you don't want reverted should first be copied off the virtual drive into a host folder—say, the Documents folder in the Home folder on your Mac.

Backing Up a Fusion VM

Although Fusion offers no way to clone a virtual machine, the structure of a Fusion virtual machine makes it simple to back up.

In Parallels Desktop, a virtual machine is comprised of multiple files. For example, a separate file makes up the VM's virtual RAM, and another file serves as its hard drive. But in VMware Fusion, there's just one file. All you need to do is make a copy of that file, and store it in a location other than your computer's primary hard drive.

The file is located in the Documents folder, in a subfolder labeled Virtual Machines. Simply copy this file to another location. If you are using Time Machine in Leopard, any changes made to the VM file will be part of that backup feature's record. Time Machine may be your best bet for an easy Fusion VM backup. I'll go into more detail about Time Machine in Chapter 10.

Using Fusion with Boot Camp

Chapter 2 focused on installing Windows using Boot Camp, which lets you switch between Windows and Mac OS X at startup. But as with Parallels Desktop, you don't have to choose between Fusion and Boot Camp. You can put the Boot Camp partition to work as a virtual machine in VMware Fusion. That way, when you start Fusion and go to the Virtual Machine Library, it will detect the presence of a Boot Camp partition and add it automatically to the list of available VMs. How cool is that?

There are some caveats, however. You can't suspend a virtual machine that uses a Boot Camp partition, nor can you use the Snapshot feature with it. And because you're using the same Windows installation relied upon by Boot Camp, if you make changes, such as adding files or folders, installing or removing software, or tweaking settings, they will also appear when you boot directly into Windows using Boot Camp. Conversely, if you make a change to Windows while booted directly into it via Boot Camp, that change will show up when you run that Windows installation as a virtual machine.

To set up a Boot Camp partition as a virtual machine:

1. Launch Fusion. The Boot Camp partition should appear in your Virtual Machine Library (**FIGURE 8.3**).

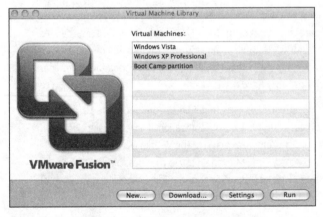

FIGURE 8.3 A Boot Camp partition should automatically appear in your Virtual Machine Library list. If it's not there right away, wait a few seconds.

2. Select the partition and click Run. The Mac OS X system password prompt appears.

3. Enter your system password and press Enter. A system message appears indicating that Fusion is preparing the Boot Camp partition to run as a virtual machine. When completed, the new VM will launch in Fusion.

   As part of the initial launch, VMware Tools will install automatically.

4. You may or may not be prompted to restart the VM. If you are, choose the restart option.

When the process is complete, you'll have a working VM that uses the Boot Camp partition for its Windows installation.

Exploring VMware Importer

If you've been using Parallels Desktop and created a Windows virtual machine, you may have a lot invested in that installation. You may have installed software and configured Windows just the way you like it. VMware Transporter lets you convert an existing Parallels VM into one usable by VMware Fusion.

At this writing, VMware Transporter is beta software, and is available at this writing from www.vmware.com/download/fusion/importer_tool.html.

To convert a Parallels VM to a Fusion VM:

1. Download VMware Importer, which is saved to your Mac as a ZIP file. It will be saved to your Downloads folder, or wherever your browser directs Web downloads. Go to the Downloads folder and double-click the ZIP file. VMware Importer will be extracted into the folder.

2. Double-click VMware Importer. The program opens.

3. Navigate to Documents > Parallels on your hard drive and find the folder containing the virtual machine you want to convert. Drag and drop it onto the VMware Importer window.

 TIP

As with Parallels, using the Boot Camp-installed version of Windows Vista presents some challenges with that operating system's activation scheme. If you have already activated Vista after booting directly into the partition, you may be required to activate it again the first time you launch it n the VM. However, if VMware Tools installed correctly, you should only be asked to do this once.

TIP

VMware also has a free tool that lets you convert a physical PC to a virtual machine. VMware Converter Starter Edition runs on your Windows PC and converts the drive and software configuration into a file that can be used as a VM for Fusion. It works best with Windows XP—at this writing, its support for Windows Vista is described as "experimental" by VMware. You can download it at www.vmware.com/download/converter/.

4. Click the Convert button. A dialog box asks where you want to save the VM. The default is the Virtual Machines folder in the Documents folder. Click Save.

The conversion process begins (**FIGURE 8.4**).

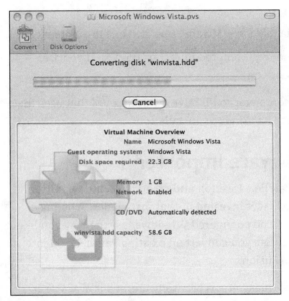

FIGURE 8.4 Converting a Parallels VM to a Fusion VM will take some time.

The conversion will take some time, depending on the size of the VM's hard drive. When it's finished, a completion notice appears.

5. Click Quit to exit, Convert Another to import another Parallels VM into Fusion, or Run Virtual Machine to launch the converted VM.

Because this is a copy of the Parallels VM, it will have all the settings and identifiers of the original. That means if you try to run both the Parallels and Fusion versions of the VM at the same time, there may be conflicts, such as duplicate MAC addresses on your network. You'll need to reactivate Windows, as it will see the change to Fusion as being new virtual hardware.

part II

Macintosh for Windows Users

chapter 9

Mac Basics

Kyrie O'Connor, the *Houston Chronicle's* deputy managing editor for features, is sharp, but the first to admit she's hapless when it comes to technology.

When she told me she'd bought a MacBook, I was delighted. I sat with her as she went through the setup process.

"Oh!" she said after a bit. "This is speaking my language!"

"What do you mean?" I asked.

"It talks to me like I'm an idiot!"

Of course, she's not and it doesn't. The Mac presents computing in a way that makes sense to her, even though she's a longtime Windows user.

This chapter explains the similarities and differences between Windows and Mac. In the end, you'll know your taskbar from your Dock, your Explorer from your Finder. And you won't feel like an idiot in the process.

NOTE

This chapter is not
meant to be an exhaus-
tive manual for Mac
OS X. Think of it
instead as a simple
translation between
slightly different
languages. For more
details, I heartily
recommend Robin
Williams' excellent
Mac OS X 10.5 Leopard:
Peachpit Learning Series.

Using the Mouse and Keyboard

Most users interact with any computer via the mouse and keyboard, and
if you've been using a computer for any length of time, you'll find their
layouts to be quite similar.

But differences in the operating system and computing philosophy translate into some important differences in the keyboard and mouse as well,
many of which have traditionally confused Windows users who sit down
at a Mac for the first time.

Let's examine these differences in detail.

Keying It In

At first glance, Mac keyboards have a familiar look.

Most computer keyboards have a series of function keys across the top
that, when pressed, perform specific tasks. In some cases, these keys can
be programmed to do different things. The bulk of the keys in the middle
are the letter and number keys used for typing. The keys at the bottom
of the layout traditionally are used for navigation and for changing the
function of what other keys might do. Full-size keyboards also have
additional navigation keys and a numeric keypad to the right.

The functionality of Macintosh keyboards varies based on whether they're
designed for portable or desktop systems, and how old they are. For the
purposes of this exercise, we'll look at Apple's wireless keyboard, which
was introduced with the aluminum iMac line in mid-2007 (**FIGURE 9.1**).

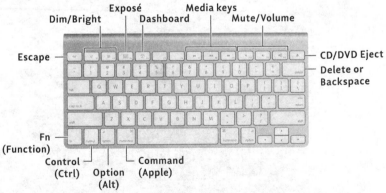

FIGURE 9.1 The wireless Mac keyboard released in mid-2007 is based on the
keyboard used in Apple's MacBook notebook line.

Top keys

The keys running along the top row are function keys, also known as FKeys. What they do varies based on the kind of Mac you're using. They're different for this keyboard, which is designed for a desktop computer, than you might see on a MacBook or MacBook Pro.

The FKeys include:

- **Esc.** Also known as the Escape key, Esc is used to exit many operations. For example, if you choose File > Save in a word processor to display a dialog box for saving a file, pressing Esc is the same as clicking the Cancel button and will close the box without saving the file.

- **Dim** and **Bright.** Controls the screen's brightness level. This is particularly useful on a notebook, as dimming the screen can extend battery life.

- **Exposé.** Instantly arranges multiple open windows on the desktop, making it easier to find what you're looking for.

- **Dashboard.** Invokes a group of widgets that provide specific bits of information, such as a clock, current weather, stock quotes, and a dictionary search. I'll talk more about Dashboard in Chapter 12.

- **Media keys.** These keys—forward, pause/play, and reverse—control the functions of your media player, which most likely is iTunes.

- **Mute** and **Volume.** These keys control the sound levels on your Mac: mute, decrease volume, and increase volume. The increase and decrease buttons make cute little water-drop sounds

- **CD/DVD Eject.** Pressing this key ejects a disk from your Mac's CD or DVD drive.

- **Delete.** On Mac notebook keyboards (and this keyboard), there's only one Delete key, and it's the Backspace key. On desktop Macs with a full-sized keyboard, there's a forward-delete (labeled Delete) key in the cluster of keys between the main keyboard and the numeric keypad. You can get the Delete/Backspace key to perform a forward-delete by holding down the Fn key while pressing the Delete key.

Bottom keys

The lower keys tagged in Figure 9.1 are modifier keys that are used in conjunction with other keys. If you press one of these keys by themselves, nothing will happen. However, if you hold one of them down while pressing another key, it will change the behavior of the key you press. For example, pressing and holding Command + C while pressing V will paste the contents of the Mac's clipboard into the current document.

Here are the bottom keys and their functions:

- **Fn.** Also known as the Function key. On PC notebook keyboards, this key is often used to handle secondary key functions, such as screen brightness or volume. Some PC notebooks use it along with letter keys to simulate a numeric keypad. On the Mac, though, it's generally used to modify the Function keys at the top of the keyboard, though it may be used to change the behavior of other keys as well.

- **Control.** Labeled Ctrl on Mac notebooks, it's the cause of much confusion for many Windows users. On Windows keyboards, Control + C, V, and X are used to respectively copy, paste, and cut text and images. But on the Mac, the Command key is used instead.

- **Option.** Also labeled as Alt on most modern Macs, this is the equivalent of the Alt key on Windows systems.

- **Command.** Also known as the Apple key. On Mac notebooks, this key is labeled with two icons: Apple's logo and the ⌘ symbol. This is considered the main modifier key, and is used frequently in Mac keyboard commands. The closest equivalent to this is the Windows key, though pressing the Windows key by itself brings up the Start menu.

TIP

If you're working in Windows in either Parallels Desktop for Mac or VMware Fusion, either Command or Control will invoke the traditional copy, paste, and cut commands.

Key combo equivalents

While the mouse has become the primary way most folks navigate graphically-based operating systems such as Windows and Mac, many people still use key combinations to get things done. Here's a list of the most common ones in Windows, and how they translate to a Mac keyboard.

TABLE 9.1 Window and Mac Keyboard Shortcuts

Actions	Windows	Mac
Copy to the clipboard	Control + C	Command + C
Cut to the clipboard	Control + X	Command + X
Paste to the clipboard	Control + V	Command + V
Shut down a program	Alt + F4	Command + Q

continues on next page

continued from previous page

TABLE 9.1 Window and Mac Keyboard Shortcuts

Actions	Windows	Mac
Kill nonresponsive program	Control + Alt + Del	Command + Option + Escape
Select multiple items	Alt-click	Control-click
Select all	Control + A	Command + A
Properties	Alt + Enter	Command + I
Toggle through running programs	Alt + Tab	Command + Tab
Save	Control + S	Command + S
Open	Control + O	Command + O
Close	Control + W	Command + W
Print	Control + P	Command + P

Mousing Around

For years, an Apple mouse had just one button, the equivalent of a left-click on a two-button Windows mouse. In the holy wars between operating system true believers, this was a serious issue of almost spiritual proportions.

Windows users argued that a multi-button mouse was more user friendly, allowing for context menus without also having to hold down a key while clicking. Mac users countered that a one-button mouse was more intuitive, and that most folks didn't use the right-mouse button when it was available anyway.

Of course, Mac users have long been able to connect a multi-button mouse with full support for right-clicking to their systems. And the argument was laid to rest in 2005, when Apple began selling its first two-button mouse, the Mighty Mouse. Today, all Macs are sold with a Mighty Mouse, which is available in both wired and wireless versions. In fact, the Mighty Mouse now has a lot more than two buttons.

Getting that right-click feeling

But in a nod to its one-button past, by default Apple sets both the left and right buttons to be a left-click, also known as the primary button. If you're a Windows user, you'll have to change the right button to be the secondary button, which generates a right-click.

To change the mouse settings:

1. From the Apple menu, choose System Preferences.

2. In the System Preferences window, click Keyboard & Mouse to display the Keyboard & Mouse dialog window.

3. Select the Mouse item at the top of the screen. The Mouse dialog window appears (**FIGURE 9.2**).

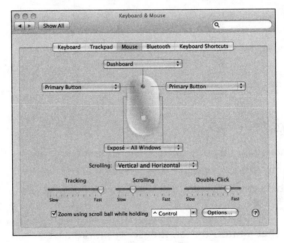

FIGURE 9.2 Look at all those buttons! This is not your father's average Apple mouse.

4. Click the Primary Button dropdown menu on the right and select Secondary Button.

   Note the various other buttons you can program. The scroll ball between the left and right buttons is a button; there are two pressure-sensitive pads on either side of the Mighty Mouse that, when pressed at the same time, will invoke Exposé. In essence, this is a four-button mouse.

5. To close the Keyboard & Mouse window, click the red button in the upper left.

Right-clicking on a Mac notebook keyboard

But what if you have a MacBook or MacBook Pro? These portables have a trackpad with a single button beneath them. Without adding a traditional mouse, how can you do a right-click?

The Mac operating system has an extremely cool feature that turns a two-finger tap on the trackpad into a right-click. This is one of my favorite things about Mac notebooks, and I've become so used to it that I find myself two-finger-clicking on the trackpads of Windows notebooks out of habit.

This feature also enables you to tap on an object with a single finger to simulate a left-click. If you don't turn it on, you must use the trackpad's mouse button for left-clicking.

To set up two-finger tapping on a Mac portable:

1. Follow Steps 1 and 2 in the previous exercise to display the Keyboard & Mouse dialog window.

2. Select the Trackpad item at the top of the window, and the Trackpad pane displays (**FIGURE 9.3**).

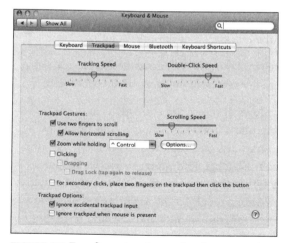

FIGURE 9.3 Two-finger tapping can be all yours just by configuring this pane.

3. Select the Clicking option. When this option is selected, the option "For secondary clicks, place two fingers on the trackpad then click the button" changes to "Tap trackpad using two fingers for secondary click." Once it changes, select the option.

4. If you'd like to be able to click an item on the screen and then hold your finger on the trackpad and drag the item to a new location, select the Dragging option.

5. Click the red button at the top of the window to close the Keyboard & Mouse window.

Now let's use your newfound keyboard and mousing skills to navigate the basics of the Mac operating system.

Exploring the Desktop and the Finder

Just as the desktop and Windows Explorer are at the heart of Windows, the desktop and the Finder are the core of the Mac OS X experience. They are the components that let you navigate through your programs, as well as the documents those programs create.

Both the Windows and Mac operating systems use the same metaphor: documents sitting on a desktop, opened and viewed through windows and folders. Because of these similarities, most folks who learn one of these operating systems have an easy time navigating the other.

What's on the Desktop?

Let's start by examining the Macintosh desktop (**FIGURE 9.4**).

It is, as you can see, quite similar to the Windows desktop. Here's a quick inventory of the major components, and what each does:

- **Desktop.** Like the Windows desktop, the equivalent in the Mac is the center of your computer's universe. You can drag documents to it; drop aliases (a.k.a. shortcuts on Windows) to common files and programs; and change the background image (a.k.a. wallpaper on Windows). But it also serves the same purpose as the My Computer folder in Windows, providing quick access to your hard drive, any CDs or DVDs you've inserted into an optical drive, and any network or removable disks you've connected to your Mac.

- **Menu bar.** In Windows, each application has its own menu. On the Mac, there's one menu bar running across the top of the desktop, and its menu items morph depending on which program is in use at the time. On the right side of the menu bar are icons that provide important information about your system.

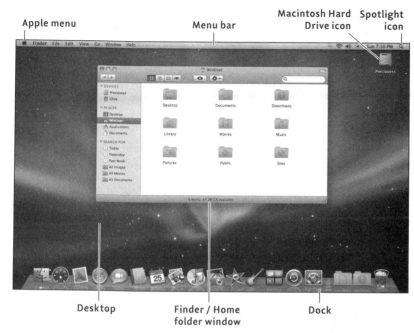

FIGURE 9.4 This is a "virgin" Mac OS X Leopard desktop as you might see it after booting up your Mac for the first time.

- **Apple menu.** This is the constant in the menu bar, providing quick access to information about your system, programs, and documents that you've recently accessed, the System Preferences (a.k.a. the Control Panel in Windows), and the Sleep/Restart/Shutdown functions. It doesn't change regardless of the program in use.

- **Spotlight.** This is the equivalent of the search field in the Windows Vista Start menu. It lets you quickly find programs and documents by entering keywords.

- **Macintosh Hard Drive icon.** This is just like the C drive icon within My Computer on Windows. It gives you direct access to the folders and files on your drive.

- **Finder / Home Folder window.** The Finder's equivalent in Windows is Windows Explorer. It can be viewed in different ways. Here, it's shown via the Home folder, which is akin to the user folder in Windows Vista, or the My Documents folder in Windows XP.

- **Dock.** The Dock is like a cross between the Windows Start menu and the taskbar. It contains icons for programs you use often, folders you access frequently, and programs that are currently running.

The desktop is your working space on the Mac. It's "You Central," just as it is in Windows. From here you can get to all the other components mentioned above. Other parts of the Mac operating system all link back to it in some way.

Optical drive magic

Any drives that you connect to your Mac, from a thumb drive to a USB-based external hard disk, to a shared network drive, are displayed on the desktop in the same way as the Macintosh Hard Drive icon.

For example, all Macs have an optical drive—a CD or, more likely these days, a DVD burner—but you don't see that drive anywhere until there's actually a disk inserted in it. When you do, it appears on your desktop.

1. Insert a CD or DVD into your Mac's optical drive. An icon of an optical disk appears on your desktop (**FIGURE 9.5**).

FIGURE 9.5 You won't know your optical drive is even there until you insert a disk.

2. Double-click the drive to open it. If it's an installation disk for software, it will open on its own to display the installer. If it's an audio CD, iTunes will launch automatically.

3. To eject the disk, press and hold the Eject button on the keyboard, or drag the CD/DVD icon to the Trash on the Dock.

Redecorating your desktop

Just as you can in Windows, you can right-click or Control-click the Mac desktop to display a menu that lets you customize your desktop, organize icons, create folders, and set view options (**FIGURE 9.6**).

FIGURE 9.6 Right-click or Control-click the desktop to display this context menu.

Want to change the background image? Try this:

1. Right-click or Control-click the desktop to display the context menu.

2. Select Change Desktop Background. The Desktop & Screen Saver dialog window appears (**FIGURE 9.7**).

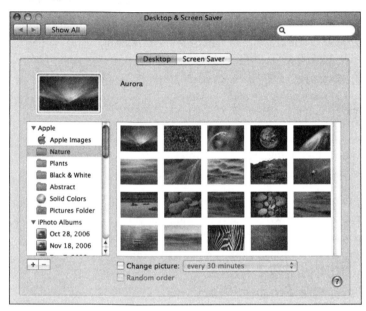

FIGURE 9.7 Choose an image from this collection to be your cool new desktop background.

3. Click any image and it immediately becomes your background. Use the menu on the left to navigate through different folders, each of which has its own set of images. When you're finished, close the Desktop & Screensaver window by clicking the red button in the upper left.

The desktop is actually a component of the Finder. Remember I mentioned that the menu bar changes depending on which application is active? When you click the desktop, the name of the active program in the menu bar switches to Finder.

Getting organized on the desktop

You can use the desktop to hold files and folders, just as you can in Windows. Drag files out of folders and drop them on the desktop. You can also create new folders in a process similar to that used in Windows:

1. Right-click or Control-click the open desktop to see the context menu.

2. Choose New Folder. A folder labeled Untitled Folder appears on the desktop, with the title area highlighted (**FIGURE 9.8**).

FIGURE 9.8 When a new folder is created on the Mac, you can instantly begin typing in a name for it.

3. Type the folder's new name and press Enter. Now you can drag the folder to a permanent spot on your desktop.

If you double-click that folder to open it, the Finder window displays. Simply put, the Finder window is a container for your files and subfolders. But it's also a powerful way to navigate your Mac. You can get to almost any other part of your Mac from the Finder window.

What's in the Finder Window?

Mac users know that the Finder is a large window in which they locate programs and documents. The Finder window is the equivalent of folder windows in Windows Explorer. And as is the case with Explorer, particularly with its enhancements in Windows Vista, you can use the Finder window to access almost anything on or connected to your computer.

 TIP

Despite the Home folder's name, don't go looking for a folder with that label on it. The Home folder uses the short user name you entered when you first set up your Mac, along with an icon that looks like a house 🏠.

Get to Know the Home Folder Window

Once you've logged into your account on your Mac, you can most easily get to both your programs and documents via the Home folder.

To get to the Home folder:

1. Locate the Finder icon on the Dock (**FIGURE 9.9**).

FIGURE 9.9 The Finder icon is the happy guy usually found on the far left of the Dock.

2. Click the icon. The Home folder opens.

Wow, there's a lot going on here, and now you can see where Apple gets the name "Finder" (**FIGURE 9.10**). From any folder, you can get to just about any other device, folder, file, or network location on your Mac.

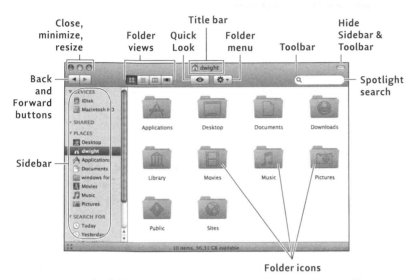

Close, minimize, resize — Folder views — Quick Look — Title bar — Folder menu — Toolbar — Hide Sidebar & Toolbar

Back and Forward buttons — Sidebar — Spotlight search — Folder icons

FIGURE 9.10 Finder folders are busy places, providing access to devices, files, network locations, and other key folders.

What you see here isn't confined to the Home folder; all the folder and other windows available via the Finder window have these features. Let's look at the components of a folder in the Finder window.

The first thing you might notice are the Folder icons. These are the sub-folders within the Home folder. They're similar in some respects to the various data subfolders in Vista's Documents folder (Movies, Music, Pictures, and so on.). The images on the icons give you a clue as to what they hold.

Another major component is the sidebar, a handy gateway to all the other areas of your Mac. If you can get to any Finder window, you can get to all of the other areas from here. The sidebar is the equivalent of the navigation pane in Windows Vista.

NOTE

There are some important differences between the Close/Minimize/Resize buttons in the Mac and their Windows equivalents. In Windows, clicking the red X button closes folder windows, and if you click that X in a program window, it will shut down the program. In the Mac, clicking the Close button in a program only kills the *active window*—it does NOT shut down the program itself. To do that, you'll need to click the program's name in the menu bar, and then choose Quit from the menu that appears.

Also, although you might think the Resize button would be equal to Windows' Maximize button, it doesn't usually do that. To make a window full-screen on a Mac, you'll need to either manually resize it (I'll tell you how later in this chapter), or, with some programs, from the menu bar you can choose View > Full Screen.

The sidebar has four different headings, each signifying a different component of your computer:

- **Devices.** Here you'll find any hardware component connected to your computer. If you're backing up your computer to Apple's iDisk service, you'll find that here, too.

- **Shared.** These are shared drives and folders from other computers on your network. Clicking on any of these will give you quick access to the files on those networked systems.

- **Places.** These primarily are folders and mounted network drives on your computer. You can drag any folder or network share here to provide quick access. To remove it, just drag the icon off the sidebar and it will vanish.

- **Search For.** The icons here are called Smart Folders, and they're predefined searches. You can add other searches as Smart Folders (for example, any document containing your name). I'll detail this feature in Chapter 11 as a part of Spotlight.

Perhaps the most critical component of the Finder window is the toolbar, which runs across the top of the Finder window and features various buttons and fields for working with the Finder. It includes the following:

- **Back and Forward buttons.** These are just like the Back and Forward buttons in a Web browser, allowing you to quickly move to previous or subsequent folders as you navigate the Finder. (These buttons are also found in Explorer windows.)

- **Close/Minimize/Resize.** These buttons are similar to the familiar buttons found on the upper right of every Windows folder, but they're on the upper left here, and they behave a little differently. The red button on the left closes the window. The amber button in the middle minimizes the window to an icon on the Dock. The green button on the right resizes the window; clicking it once will either enlarge or reduce it; clicking it again returns the window to its default size.

- **Folder views.** Controls how the contents of folders are displayed. I'll go into more detail on this later in this section.

- **Folder menu.** Provides access to options for configuring and customizing the folder.

- **Quick Look.** Clicking this button gives you a quick preview of documents, images, and multimedia files. I'll detail this more later in this chapter.

- **Title bar.** Reflects the name of the folder. As mentioned earlier in this chapter, the house icon tells you it's also the Home folder.

- **Spotlight search.** This lets you search for anything on your Mac, from programs to documents. I'll detail this more in Chapter 11.

- **Hide Toolbar & Sidebar.** Want to maximize the screen real estate of the active Finder window to show mostly files and folders? Clicking this button quickly gets rid of the toolbar and the sidebar. Click it a second time to restore them.

Other Important Folders

Some folders are more important than others in Mac OS X, just as they are in Windows. There are a handful of them that are useful to be aware of and to understand how they work:

 Applications. This folder is similar to the Programs folder in Windows, with one key difference. In Windows, Programs holds shortcuts to the software executable files, while in the Mac, what you see in the Applications folders are the executables themselves. In many cases, installing software for the Mac requires dragging a piece of software into this folder. More on this in Chapter 11.

 Downloads. By default, Apple's Web browser directs files downloaded from the Internet into this folder, which is located inside the Home folder. The Downloads folder also sits out on the Dock. There's also a Downloads folder in Windows Vista, while in Windows XP, downloads are typically saved to the desktop by default.

 Documents. Most applications will save their files to this folder, and some will create subfolders here. In previous chapters dealing with Parallels Desktop for Mac and VMware Fusion, I mentioned that both of these programs store their virtual machine files in subfolders in the Documents folder. Documents is another folder that, by default, sits on the Dock. Documents has its Windows equivalent in the Documents folder in Vista and My Documents in Windows XP.

Public. If you choose to share files over a network, this is the folder that is initially visible to others. Inside it is another folder, the Drop Box, where those who connect to your Mac can leave files for you. There's a Public Folder in Vista, and a Shared Documents folder in XP.

Utilities. Located inside the Applications folder, the Utilities folder holds important system-level applications, such as the Keychain, which lets you manage passwords, and Network Utility, which can help troubleshoot Internet connection issues. The Utilities folder is similar to the System Tools folder in Windows.

There are also several folders whose names aptly describe what they hold: Pictures, Music, and Movies. You can find them in the Home folder.

Seeing the Finder in Different Ways

The view of the Finder window shown earlier in this chapter is the default view, with folders and files shown as icons. Just as Windows Explorer lets you see objects in different views, so can the Finder. In fact, you can look at the contents of your folders in three other ways.

FIGURE 9.11 shows four buttons labeled Folder Views. Clicking any one of those will change the way items appear in the Finder window.

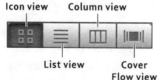

FIGURE 9.11 Clicking on these buttons, which are in the Folder sidebar, changes the way folders and files are shown in the Finder.

You've already seen Icon view. Let's take a look at the others.

List view

Click the second button in the row to see your files and folders in a list (**FIGURE 9.12**).

Exploring the Desktop and the Finder | 127

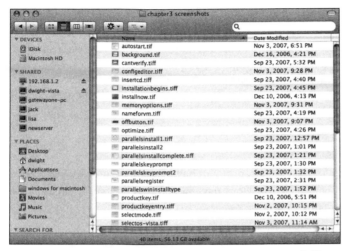

FIGURE 9.12 The List view provides plenty of details about each file and folder.

Use this view when you want to quickly sort files by name, date modified, file size, and file type. It lets you see a lot of files even in a small window. This is almost identical to the Details view in Windows Explorer.

Column view

If you click the third button, the view switches to show a Column display similar to the List, but with added benefits (**FIGURE 9.13**).

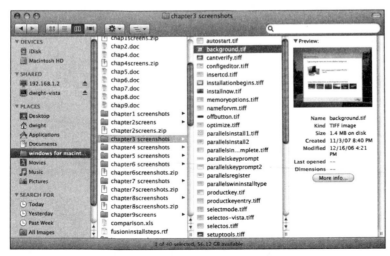

FIGURE 9.13 Column view shows you both the folder you're in, as well as the contents of the folder it's in.

Use this view when you're working in nested folders and want to see both what's in the current folder, as well as its parent. It helps with navigation, showing you where you are in relation to other folders, and thus is very useful when browsing networked computers.

In addition, the right-most column by default will display a preview of a document when you click it.

Cover Flow view

If you've used iTunes before, or if you have an iPhone or the iPod Touch, then you've seen the Cover Flow view, which is activated by clicking the fourth button (**FIGURE 9.14**).

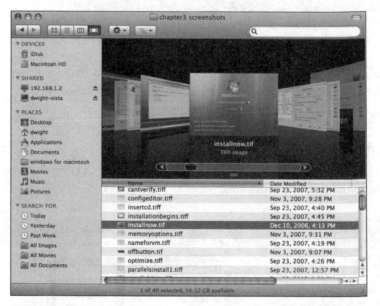

FIGURE 9.14 The Cover Flow view gives you a graphical presentation of your files and folders.

Cover Flow provides a slick, gallery-style preview pane at the top of the folder. You can use the slider underneath the image to browse them, or simply click a file in the list view below.

Cover Flow is best used with folders that have documents, images, or media files, because it lets you see at a glance what the file's all about. For example, if it's a Word document, you'll see its first page. If it's a JPG, you'll see a thumbnail image.

See It Quick Using Quick Look

Cover Flow is one of two very graphical enhancements Apple made to the Finder as part of Leopard. The other, which is just as cool, is called Quick Look. It gives you a quick, simple preview of a file simply by pressing the space bar.

The file can either be in a Folder window or on the desktop. Simply click the file, then press the space bar or the Quick Look icon on the Finder window toolbar, and a Quick Look preview window jumps front and center (FIGURE 9.15).

FIGURE 9.15 If Quick Look knows what a document is, it will display a preview of it when you press the space bar.

Quick Look can display documents and images. It can also play video and audio files. But it must "know" about the file in order to display it. Quick Look has a plug-in system that lets developers give the feature the ability to display many file types. At this writing, there are only a handful of them. Use your favorite Internet search engine to hunt for "Quick Look plugins."

Getting Docked

Of all the features in the Mac OS X interface, the Dock is my favorite. It is simple and elegant and designed to do one thing: Make your computing life a lot easier.

For Windows users, the best way to think of the Dock is that it is a combination of the Windows taskbar and the Start menu. It both highlights the programs that are actively running and provides a way to quickly access programs and folders you use often.

Let's take a look at the Dock (**FIGURE 9.16**). Note that what you're seeing is not the default, "out of the box" version of the Dock you get on a new Mac. I've changed some things to make some points.

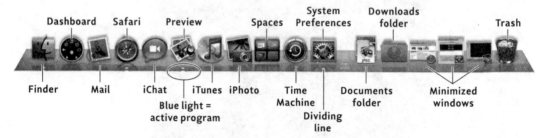

FIGURE 9.16 The Dock provides instant access to frequently used programs and folders.

I'll go into details about many of the applications you see on the left side of the Dock's dividing line in Chapter 12. For this chapter, I'll focus on managing programs and customizing the Dock.

One important feature to note is the dividing line, which in Figure 9.16 appears between the System Preferences and the Documents folder. Program icons go on the left side of the line; folders, documents and minimized windows go on the right.

Clicking on a program icon once on the left side launches the program; you don't need to double-click. Clicking on a folder on the right side invokes the Dock's Stacks feature, which I'll detail later in this chapter. Clicking on a window that's been minimized to the right side of the Dock restores the window to the desktop.

Making the Dock Your Own

The Dock is highly customizable. You can add or remove icons, adjust its size, change how it reacts when you mouse over it, and even change where it sits on the desktop.

Adding new icons

For example, normally icons for iCal, Apple's calendar program, and the Address Book appear by default on the Dock. I don't use those programs, so I've simply clicked on them and dragged the icons off the Dock, at which point they vanish in a puff of cartoon smoke.

Adding icons for folders and programs is just as easy:

- Double-click the hard drive icon on the desktop. The drive's Finder window opens.

- Double-click the Applications folder; another Finder window opens, revealing the programs on your Mac.

- Choose one of the programs, click and hold on it, and drag the icon to the desired position on the left side of the Dock's dividing line. The icons that are already there will part slightly; drop the new program icon where you want it.

- To add a folder or document to the right side of the divider, repeat the process with the file or folder of your choice.

Tweaking the Dock

You can change many aspects of the Dock via System Preferences. To adjust how the Dock looks and behaves:

1. Click the System Preferences icon on the Dock, and then click the Dock item in the collection of preferences.

   or

   Right-click or Control-click the dividing line and choose Dock Preferences from the menu that appears.

 TIP

You actually don't have to open the Dock's preferences to resize the Dock. Just click and hold on the dividing line, and then move your mouse back and forth to adjust the size. Release when the size is to your liking.

The Dock dialog window appears (**FIGURE 9.17**).

FIGURE 9.17 The Dock dialog window gives you the power to change the Dock's size, position, and behavior.

2. To change the size of the Dock, adjust the Size slider.

3. Select the Magnification option to have the Dock's icons grow in size as you mouse over them. This makes them easier to see and select, particularly if you shrink the size of the dock to accommodate a large number of icons. Use the slider to determine just how big they grow.

4. Select one of the three Position on Screen radio buttons—Left, Bottom, or Right—to choose where the Dock sits on your desktop.

5. Click the Minimize Using dropdown arrow to control the animation used when minimizing and restoring windows. When set to Genie Effect, the default windows appear to shrink in size from the bottom up, like a genie going into its bottle, as they minimize. The Scale Effect is more like that found in Windows Vista or XP, in which windows appear to collapse in on themselves as they minimize.

6. Leave the Animate Opening Applications option selected to have icons on the dock bounce when they are launching. Deselect this option if you don't want them to bounce.

7. Select Automatically Hide and Show the Dock if you want the Dock to only be visible when you move your mouse cursor to its vicinity. This is similar to autohiding the taskbar in Windows.

8. Click the red button in the left corner of the Dock dialog window to close it.

NOTE

If you move the Dock away from the bottom of the screen, it will lose the reflective shelf and 3D look that was introduced with Leopard. When placed on the left or right sides of the screen, the Dock looks more like it did in Tiger (OS X 10.4), with the icons flush against a neutral background. Note also that you cannot put the dock at the top of the screen because the menu bar is there.

All About Stacks

One of the most visually interesting—and most controversial—features in Leopard is Stacks, which is a new way of displaying what's inside the folder parked on the Dock. In Tiger, the previous version of Mac OS X, clicking folders on the Dock brought up a Finder window. But with Stacks, what's inside a folder gets displayed in one of two ways:

If only a few items are in a folder, Stacks shows the icons in a display called a Fan (**FIGURE 9.18**). The display looks like a "jet" of icons shooting up from the folder and curving slightly to the right.

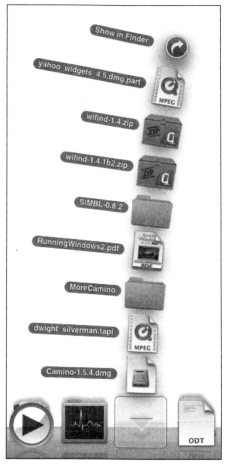

FIGURE 9.18 The Fan view in Stacks appears only when just a few items are in a folder.

However, if there are many items in a folder, icons are displayed in an attractive, 3D layout called the Grid (**FIGURE 9.19**).

FIGURE 9.19 If you have many items in the folder, Stacks displays them in a grid.

Both views still let you see the folder items in Finder if you click the Show in Finder icon.

Stacks has generated some dissent among longtime Apple users who question its value, since it requires an additional click to see the items in a standard Finder window. In addition, if there are a lot of icons in a folder, the labels under the icons may be truncated as the icons are pushed closer together, making it hard to see what each one is called.

But for those who do appreciate eye candy, here's a tip: Try Shift-clicking a folder on the Dock for a very cool, slow-motion display as the folder opens up.

Now that you know how to navigate the Mac operating system, let's look at some of its more advanced features.

chapter 10

Inside System Preferences

System Preferences is to the Mac operating system what the Control Panel is to Windows. It's one-stop shopping for nearly all your operating system tweaking needs. You may need to dip into the Utilities folder from time to time, but for the most part, System Preferences is where you'll spend most of your time fiddling with settings (**FIGURE 10.1**, next page).

We've already delved into System Preferences in other parts of this book. In Chapter 4, we used it to enable Spaces. In Chapter 9, we used it to set up right-clicking in the mouse and to change the desktop background. There are more than two dozen preferences here, and more if some applications have added custom preferences. I'm not going to detail all of them, but I'll offer a brief overview of each and go into a little more detail on the most commonly used ones.

The System Preferences window groups the individual items into five categories: Personal, Hardware, Internet & Network, System, and Other.

TIP

Would you prefer to have preferences listed alphabetically? From the System Preferences menu bar, choose View > Organize Alphabetically. To revert to the original order, choose Organize by Categories.

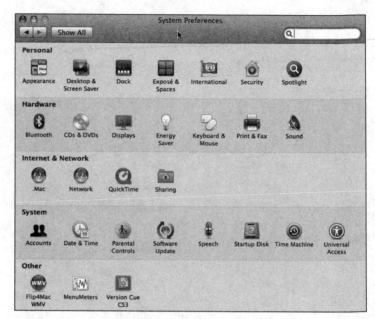

FIGURE 10.1 Need to make some change in the way the Mac works? Start here.

The Personal Group

These seven preferences primarily control how the Mac operating system looks and behaves, from appearances, to language, to security.

Appearance

Windows users often complain that the Mac operating system isn't customizable enough for their tastes, but this one preference lets you change the look of many of the Mac's features. While it doesn't match up to the features available in Windows Vista's Window Color and Appearance module, the Appearance preferences let you tweak the color of buttons, scrollbars, highlighting and some window elements; set scroll arrows together at the bottom of a window or separated at the top and bottom of the scrollbar; and change how font smoothing works.

Desktop & Screen Saver

I showed you in Chapter 9 how this preference can be used to change the desktop. You can also use it to choose a screen saver. If a saver you choose has specific options, you'll be able to set them here as well.

Dock

Also mentioned in Chapter 9, the Dock preferences control the size of the Dock, whether icons enlarge when you mouse over them, the Dock's position on the screen, and how minimizing works.

Exposé & Spaces

In Chapter 9, we visited this preference to turn on Spaces, but it does a lot more. The Exposé pane (**FIGURE 10.2**) gives you the ability to assign actions to the four corners of your Mac's screen. Moving your mouse cursor to any of these corners triggers the action, which can range from starting the screen saver, to clearing the desktop, to launching Dashboard or Spaces.

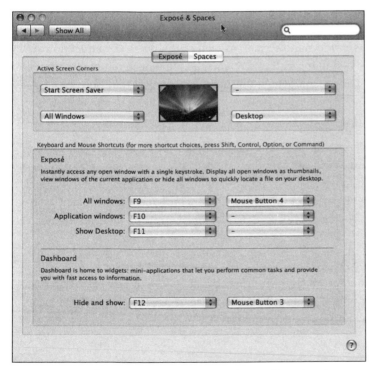

FIGURE 10.2 Configure Active Screen Corners, Spaces, Exposé, and Dashboard from the Exposé & Spaces dialog window.

Exposé & Spaces is a cool way to quickly see what's on your desktop. Use the Exposé settings to determine which keys trigger the feature's different functions. Exposé can arrange all your windows on the desktop in an orderly manner; show you all the windows related to one specific application; or clear all the windows off the desktop. Its closest parallels in Windows are the Flip 3D feature in Windows Vista and the Show Desktop icon found in the Quick Launch area of the Windows taskbar.

Finally, this preference screen also lets you assign a function key and mouse button to activate Dashboard.

International

International preferences let you change the language preferences for the Mac operating system. Unlike Windows, which requires the use of downloadable language packs, dozens of languages are built into the Mac operating system. This preference also lets you control how date and monetary formats appear, as well as the types of characters you can use when filling in forms. If you suddenly need to type traditional Chinese Zhuyin characters, this is the place to set that up.

Security

This preference is similar to Windows' Security Center. It lets you configure your Mac's network firewall; decide whether you should enter a password to access the computer; determine if the computer will lock itself after a period of inactivity; and encrypt your Home folder's contents. I'll go into more detail on Macintosh security later in Chapter 11.

Spotlight

Spotlight is the Mac's hard-drive search feature. It's so fast at finding things on your hard drive that it can also be used as a program launcher. I'll talk about this more in Chapter 11.

The Hardware Group

The preferences in the Hardware group let you manage settings for a variety of hardware devices, including printers, input devices, displays, and drives.

Bluetooth

If your Mac supports the Bluetooth wireless specification, you can use this preference to pair devices, such as mice, wireless headsets, or an iPhone, with your computer. You can also use this to create a Bluetooth network, allowing other computers to share your Internet connection.

CDs & DVDs

Use this preference to control how your Mac responds when you insert different types of disks into your computer's optical drive (**FIGURE 10.3**). For example, you can configure it to automatically open iTunes when you insert a music CD, the DVD Player when you put in a DVD, or iDVD when you insert a blank DVD.

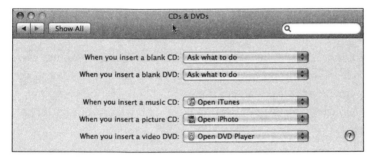

FIGURE 10.3 Here you can determine what your Mac does when a disc is put into its optical drive.

Displays

Similar to the Display Settings module in Windows, Displays provides control over brightness, screen resolution, how many colors are displayed, and color calibration. If you have multiple displays connected to your Mac, you'll be able to control these options on each screen separately, as well as determine whether the desktop is mirrored on each display.

Get That Windows Look

Some Windows users who switch to the Mac complain that the colors on the screen look "washed out." The Mac uses different color settings, but you can change them to make the display look more Windows-like. Here's how.

1. In the Displays dialog window, click the Color button at the top. The Color screen appears.

2. Click the Calibrate button, and the Display Calibrator Assistant appears.

3. Click Continue, and the Select a Target Gamma window appears.

4. Select 2.2 Television Gamma and click Continue. The Select a White Target Point screen appears.

5. Click Continue. The Give the Profile a Name screen appears.

6. Enter a name and click Continue, and then click Done.

7. Close the Displays dialog window.

Energy Saver

As with Windows, you can fine-tune how much power your computer uses, which is particularly important if your Mac is a notebook (**FIGURE 10.4**). Adjusting how long it takes before the screen blanks or the computer goes to sleep can have a significant impact on how long your battery's charge lasts.

You also can have separate settings when you're using battery or AC power. The Options button lets you show the battery status in the menu bar and determine whether the screen will dim slightly when the computer is about to go to sleep or when it is running on battery power.

Keyboard & Mouse

This preference window was introduced in Chapter 9, when I showed you how to enable right-clicking with a mouse and the trackpad. This item also controls keyboard settings, including repeat rates; shows you the battery status of connected Bluetooth devices; and lets you change keyboard shortcuts.

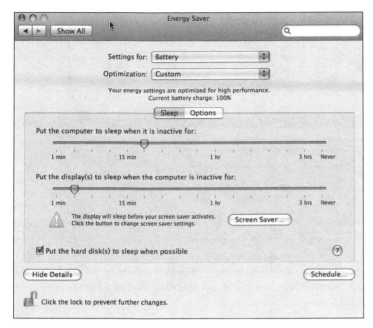

FIGURE 10.4 The Energy Saver controls a variety of power-saving options.

Print & Fax

Similar to the Printers module in the Windows Control Panel, this preference lets you manage printers and fax devices connected to your Mac. In most cases, connecting a printer is just a matter of plugging it into the Mac, but if you do need drivers, this component will help you find them. It also will let you search for printers to use on your network, including printers connected to Windows PCs. Finally, once your printer is connected and you're assigning jobs to it, you can access the print queue and manage those jobs from here.

Sound

This preference lets you change what sounds your Mac makes to notify you of system events. You can control the volume of the events separately from the overall system volume (**FIGURE 10.5**).

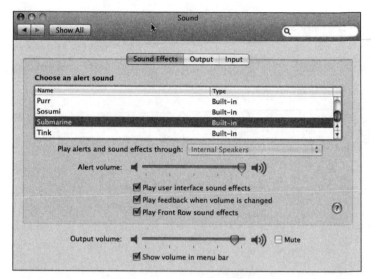

FIGURE 10.5 You can change the sound your Mac makes during a system notification here.

This screen also lets you choose which devices to use for audio input or output. For example, if you plug an external microphone into a MacBook, you can determine whether it or the built-in microphone will be the default input device.

The Internet & Network Group

The Internet & Network category may have the fewest number of preferences items, but it's one of the most important. Few Macs aren't connected to some kind of network, and almost all of them are used with Internet access of some type. Chances are good you'll spend some quality time in these areas.

.Mac

This is an online, subscription-based service offered by Apple for $99.95 a year. It allows Mac users to save up to 10 GB of files online; to control other Leopard-based Macs using the Back to My Mac feature; to synchronize calendars, bookmarks, contacts and e-mail between various Macs; and offers basic Web site hosting and a place to create photo galleries, blogs, and other Web pages. The preference window for .Mac provides statistics on how much storage remains available for your account; helps sync your computer with other Macs; and manages your offline storage on the iDisk service.

Network

This preference window, similar to the Network and Sharing Center in Windows Vista, serves as the core of your online experience on the Mac (**FIGURE 10.6**). In most cases, connecting to a network or the Internet is as simple as plugging in a cable or using a Wi-Fi connection. When you're connecting to a network that includes Windows-based PCs, though, it can be a little trickier, and this is the Mac preference window that will help you navigate those waters.

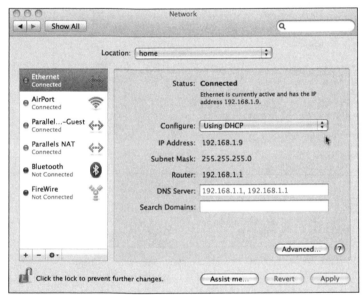

FIGURE 10.6 The Network preferences window is a central spot for controlling all your connections, be they wired or wireless.

I'll go into more detail about connecting your Mac to a network and the Internet in Chapter 11.

QuickTime

Most Windows users are going to be familiar with QuickTime, which is Apple's media player. This preference window lets you configure whether movies play automatically in your Web browser and how long video buffers before it starts playing. It also provides a way to upgrade to QuickTime Pro, which also allows you to edit media. You can also use this preference to find third-party plug-ins to extend QuickTime's capabilities.

Sharing

This is another very important preference, whose components are also similar to those found in Vista's Network and Sharing Center. It controls all the various ways you can share your Mac's resources with other computers (**FIGURE 10.7**).

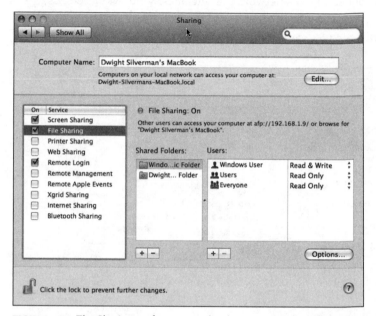

FIGURE 10.7 The Sharing preference window lets you provide different types of access to your Mac to other computers on a network.

The Sharing preference screen lets you be very specific about what others can and can't share on your Mac. You could, for example, share your printer and Internet access, but no files. Clicking on any of the services in the left pane opens a new option on the right side of the window. I'll go into this in a little more detail in the networking section of Chapter 11.

The System Group

This area serves as a catchall collection of preferences related to the basics of the Mac: date and time settings, user accounts, how the computer's software is updated, accessibility features, and so on.

Accounts

As with Windows, you can set up additional accounts on a Mac, and give users a variety of privileges. The Accounts preferences window (**FIGURE 10.8**) gives you a way to add or remove accounts, determine what programs launch when users log in, how the login menu looks when the computer starts, and whether fast user switching, also a popular feature on Windows PCs, is available.

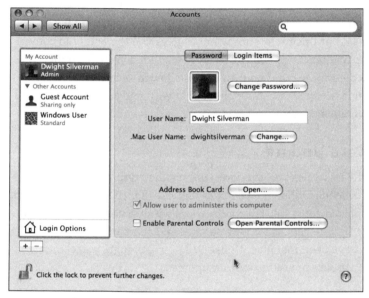

FIGURE 10.8 Set up, manage, and remove user accounts in the Accounts preferences window.

It also lets you enable the Guest account, which works differently on the Mac than it does in Windows. Here, the Guest account is temporary, existing only for as long as the guest is logged on. Once the person logs out, the structure of the account—the Home folder, settings, activity history, everything—is deleted. This ensures the integrity of your system when your niece or nephew who has a history of downloading questionable files comes to visit.

Date & Time

Set the date and time from here, or tell your Mac to get super-accurate time from the Internet. You can also change time zones, choose to display your desktop clock in digital or analog form, or even have your Mac speak the time to you in a variety of voices.

Parental Controls

Parental Controls, which are a new feature in Windows Vista, were beefed up substantially for the Mac in Leopard. I'll go into more details in Chapter 11, but this preference window gives you the ability to control what applications and Web sites are allowed for a given account. You can also determine what hours a user is allowed access to the computer, limit who a user can e-mail or chat with and set up logs to monitor your child's usage.

Software Update

This is the equivalent to Windows Update, the feature that automatically downloads and installs patches and fixes for the operating system and supported software. This preferences window controls how often Software Update checks for new patches and can show you which updates have been installed. Unlike Windows, though, you cannot uninstall Apple's operating system updates.

Speech

You can talk to your Mac, and it can talk back to you. The Speech preferences window (**FIGURE 10.9**) handles settings for both Speech Recognition (the system interprets your words and executes commands based on them) and Text-to-Speech (your Mac reads text to you in a computerized voice).

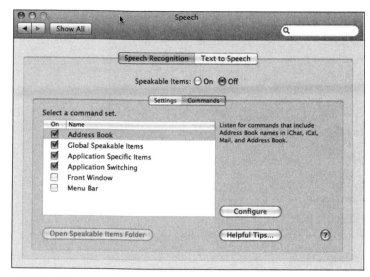

FIGURE 10.9 Want to have a conversation with your Mac? The Speech window is the place to start.

Startup Disk

Normally, you start your Mac from the hard drive and don't think twice about it. But you can connect an external drive with the Mac operating system loaded on it and boot from that instead, or boot from another computer on your network, using this preference window. If you have a Boot Camp partition, you can also select it as your boot disk from here.

Time Machine

Again, I'll talk about Time Machine more Chapter 11. This preferences window lets you pick a hard drive to which Time Machine will save your files and data. This is similar to the Backup and Restore Center in Windows Vista.

Universal Access

For those who are seeing or hearing impaired, accessibility features are controlled via the Universal Access preferences (**FIGURE 10.10**).

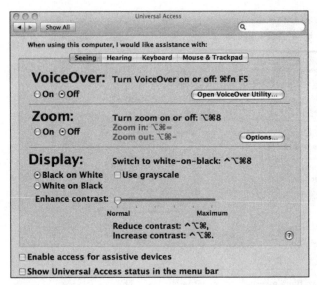

FIGURE 10.10 The Universal Access preferences window's fonts make it easy for those with seeing impairments to work with the settings.

This window lets you adjust the contrast and display for those who do not see well. For those with hearing problems, you can set the screen to flash, rather than generate a noise, on a system event. It's also where you can set up VoiceOver, a Mac feature that uses a computerized voice to describe what is happening on the screen. It also allows you to use a Braille reader with your Mac.

Other

Some programs you install may add their own preferences modules, which plug into the Other category in System Preferences. In Figure 10.6, for example, you'll find three preference items added by third-party programs. You can remove these additional items:

1. Right-click or Command-click the item in the Other category you'd like to remove. A one-item menu appears.

2. Choose Remove. You'll be prompted for an administrator's password.

3. Enter your password and click OK.

   The item disappears from the System Preferences window.

   Now that you've got some tools at your disposal, we'll work with some of Mac's more advanced features in the next chapter.

chapter 11

Advanced Mac

One of the beautiful things about Mac OS X is just how simple it is to use and learn. But scratch under the surface, and there's lots of power, too. At the risk of invoking a hokey simile, it's like a beautiful lake: You can skim along the placid surface and appreciate the view, or dive deep and explore the wonders underneath.

Whew. Now that we've gotten *that* out of the way ...

In the previous chapter, I walked you through the basics of the Mac. Now we're going to look at ways you can make your Mac, well, *your* Mac. This chapter shows you how manage applications, tweak system settings, add your Mac to your Windows network, back up your system, and get started with core Mac features, including the Dashboard, Spotlight, and Spaces.

It also addresses an issue that's always on Windows users' minds: security. As a new Mac owner, do you need to worry about viruses, Trojans, spyware, and hackers in the same way you do on a Windows PC? Read on and find out.

Managing Programs

Windows and Mac OS X each take a different approach to installing and removing programs.

In most cases, Windows programs don't store all their files in one place. Instead, during installation, parts of the program must be saved in various locations. That means nearly all Windows programs require the use of an installer to get the software onto your hard drive.

But with a Mac, installation can be as easy as dragging a single file into the Applications folder, though sometimes an installer is used. Removing Mac software can be as simple as dragging the program icon to the Trash, but in some cases you may need to run an uninstaller.

Regardless of how they get there, all Mac programs live in the Applications folder, so let's give it a quick look.

Digging Deeper in the Applications Folder

I touched briefly on the Applications folder in the previous chapter. The quickest way to get to the folder is through the hard drive icon on the desktop. But you'll access the folder enough that you'll probably want to put it on the Dock, as well.

To put the Applications folder on the Dock:

1. Double-click the Macintosh HD icon on the desktop. The drive's Finder window opens.

2. Drag the Applications folder to the area on the right side of the divider. When the items on either side of your intended Dock location part, release the icon and the Applications folder will drop into place.

3. Close the Macintosh HD folder.

For the rest of this section, I'm going to presume you've done this. Believe me, once you start using your Mac programs regularly, you'll be glad you did!

If you just click once on the Applications folder, it opens in the Stacks grid view discussed in Chapter 9. To get to a Finder window for Applications, click the Show in Finder icon in Stacks view.

Inside the Applications folder, you'll find both programs and subfolders (FIGURE 11.1).

Folder examples   Program examples

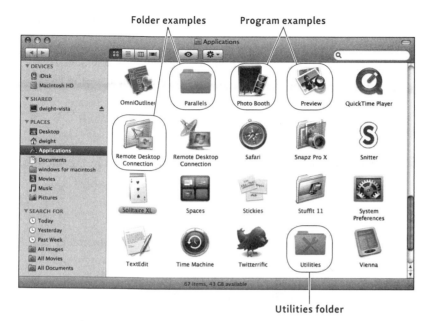

Utilities folder

FIGURE 11.1 Some programs in the Applications folder will be found inside other folders.

Notice that some folders look like, well, folders. Others are fancier, and may be so fancy they look like programs. Open them to find the programs inside.

Getting to know the Utilities folder

There's one special subfolder in Applications, and that's the Utilities folder, with the wrench-and-screwdriver icon on it (Figure 11.1). The Utilities folder and the Applications folder are considered system folders; both have designs on them to differentiate them. As mentioned in Chapter 9, the Utilities folder has programs related to the maintenance and tweaking of your Mac. Here are the most frequently used programs:

- **Activity Monitor.** Similar to the Task Manager in Windows, the Activity Monitor lets you see what programs are running and the resources they're consuming.

- **AirPort Utility.** Got an Apple AirPort Extreme wireless router? Use the Airport Utility to configure it.

- **Grab.** A new and improved utility for taking pictures of what's happening on your screen.

 TIP

Grab, while simple, has more features than a longstanding, popular feature in the Mac that lets you do screenshots with key combo commands. Command + Shift + 3 takes a picture of the entire screen. Command + Shift + 4 gives you the choice of capturing a selected region or a specific window.

- **Keychain Access.** Lets you manage passwords and security certificates.

- **Migration Assistant.** Simplifies the process of transferring settings, logins, files, and other important information from one Mac to another. This is like Windows Easy Transfer in Vista, or the File & Settings Transfer wizard in Windows XP.

- **Network Utility.** Useful for troubleshooting problems with your Internet or network connections.

- **System Profiler.** Provides detailed information about your computer, similar to the System Information application in Windows.

Adding new folders

If you install enough programs over time, the Applications folder can become cluttered. But you can make a new folder and drag program icons into it. This is not always possible in Windows, because program files may rely on other files and "lose sight" of those files if they are put elsewhere.

Let's say you have three different Web browsers on your Mac—Safari, Firefox, and Camino—and you'd like to put them in a folder named Browsers. Here's how to do it:

1. Right-click or Command-click inside the Applications folder. A context menu appears.

2. Choose New Folder. A folder labeled Untitled Folder will appear, with the label area highlighted.

3. Type the name of your new folder, in this case *Browsers*.

4. Drag the icons for Safari, Firefox, and Camino onto the Browsers folder and release them (**FIGURE 11.2**). If the folder is too full and the programs aren't within sight of the folder, dragging the program icons to the top or bottom edges of the folder will scroll the Applications folder window until you see the Browser folder.

5. Right-click or Command-click in the Applications folder and choose Clean Up to reclaim the space from consolidating the icons in one folder.

6. Open the Browser folder to confirm the icons are there, and double-click any you might like to launch.

Now that you know something about the structure of and how to use the Applications folder, let's look at how to install programs into it.

FIGURE 11.2 Drag application icons into folders to help organize them.

Installing Mac Programs

As mentioned earlier, Mac programs are installed one of two ways: by dragging the program into the Applications folder, or by running an installer. Simple programs tend to use the drag-and-drop method, while more complex applications use an installer.

Mac programs you buy at a store that come on a CD or DVD are very easy to install. Inserting the disc into the Mac's optical drive brings up a folder with a file to drag or an installer to run. But programs you download from the Internet are different, and often are confusing to Windows users.

About disk images

When you download a program, it often will come in a file format called a disk image. It's essentially a container holding the program you're going to install, but you can think of a disk image as a simulated drive.

A disk image downloads to your Mac as a file with an .img extension. Unless you've changed the default download destination, it will be saved to your Downloads folder. Disk images usually have an icon that looks like a hard drive (**FIGURE 11.3**).

FIGURE 11.3 This is the download file for Camino, an alternate Web browser.

Camino-1.5.4.dmg

When you double-click a disk image, it generates an icon similar to what you'd see if you plugged an external drive or a flash drive into a Mac's USB port (**FIGURE 11.4**).

FIGURE 11.4 When you double-click Camino's download file, it generates this icon on your desktop.

This is the disk image that contains the file. In most cases, a window may open showing you the program file or files. Here's where most Windows users get confused.

Programs that can be installed simply by dragging and dropping into the Applications folder will run from within any folder, including a disk image. Many Windows users installing Mac software for the first time see the icon inside the disk image's window and click it, thinking it's an installer, thus launching the program. Instead, you should drag the program's file into the Applications folder.

Dragging a program to install it

Let's walk through the process of installing a program you've downloaded from the Net that requires a simple drag-and-drop. We'll work with the Camino browser. (Don't worry; having Camino on your Mac won't conflict with Safari or Firefox, if you prefer either of those. It won't become your default browser unless you tell it to.)

1. Go to www.caminobrowser.org and download Camino. It should save to your Downloads folder.

2. Click the Downloads folder. Stacks will open the folder either in the Grid or Fan view. Either way, you should see the Camino download file.

3. Click the Camino download file. The Camino license agreement appears.

4. Click Accept. A progress window appears, and the Camino disk image icon materializes on the desktop. Finally, the Camino install window appears (**FIGURE 11.5**).

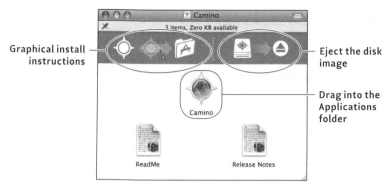

Graphical install instructions

Eject the disk image

Drag into the Applications folder

Camino

ReadMe

Release Notes

FIGURE 11.5 The Camino disk image opens to reveal the browser program and documentation.

At the top left of the window are visual instructions for installation, showing the Camino icon being dragged into the Applications folder. On the right are instructions for ejecting the disk image when you're finished. More about that in a moment.

5. Click the Camino icon and drag it into the Applications folder. A progress window appears briefly. The program is now installed.

6. Right-click or Command-click the Camino disk image on the desktop and choose Eject from the menu that appears.

   or

   Drag the disk image icon to the Trash to eject it.

   The Camino window closes.

Now, when you are ready to start Camino, just click the Applications folder in the Dock and then click the Camino icon in the Stacks grid.

Using a program installer

Large, complex programs typically use an installer. If you install something like Microsoft Office, Adobe Creative Suite, or Apple's iWork suite, you'll end up using one.

If you've been reading this book sequentially, you already know how to use an installer, because both Parallels Desktop for Mac and VMware Fusion use them. See Chapters 3 (the "Installing Parallels" section) and Chapter 6 (the "Installing Fusion" section) for instructions on using an installer.

Uninstalling Mac Programs

Removing software from your Mac is absurdly easy in most cases, regardless of whether it can be done manually or using an uninstaller.

Dragging a program to remove it

Here's how you remove most programs:

1. Open the Applications folder.

2. Click the program you want to remove and drag it to the Trash.

3. Close the Applications folder.

   You're done!

Using an uninstaller

You'll know if a program requires an uninstaller because it will be included with it. If you bought the software on a CD or DVD, you can pop the disc into the optical drive to access it.

If you downloaded the software from online, any needed uninstallers will likely be packaged in the disk image. If, when you're installing the program, you notice there's an uninstaller in the disk image folder, it's a good idea to save the file you downloaded in case you want to uninstall the program later.

Finally, when programs create their own subfolders in the Applications folder, the uninstaller will be there as well.

For this exercise, we'll remove Snapz Pro X, a screenshot program from Ambrosia Software (www.ambrosiasw.com) that creates a subfolder in the Applications folder. The uninstaller is located in the Snapz Pro subfolder, and its behavior is typical of most Mac uninstallers.

To uninstall Snapz Pro X:

1. Find the Snapz Pro X folder in the Applications folder and open it.

2. Double-click the icon labeled Snapz Pro X Uninstaller. The uninstaller launches and a confirmation window appears.

3. Click Continue. A dialog box opens with several options (**FIGURE 11.6**). In this case, you're asked whether you want to remove just Snapz Pro, an ancillary program it utilizes, or both. While these choices are

specific to Snapz Pro, this is the point during some uninstall routines at which you can make choices about how the process will proceed. In this case, we'll choose Uninstall Both.

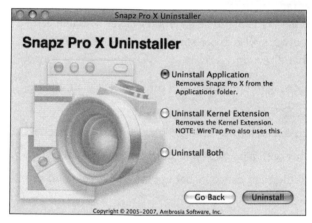

FIGURE 11.6 Some uninstall routines present you with choices to customize how programs are removed.

4. Click Uninstall. A confirmation window appears.

5. Click OK. If you are removing software that other users on your computer can access, you'll be presented with a request for your administrator password.

6. Enter your password, if prompted, and then click OK. The program is removed, and you're presented with a window indicating the uninstallation process was a success.

7. Click Quit to close the window.

Connecting to a Network and the Internet

Getting online using either Windows or Mac is fairly easy in an era of high-speed connections and almost ubiquitous Wi-Fi. Both Microsoft and Apple have streamlined the process of connection to the Internet and, for the most part, local area networks. What remains tricky in some cases is getting Macs and Windows machines to talk to each other on a network.

Chances are, if you've already got your Mac turned on and set up, it's already online. If your Mac's connected to the Internet, or can access a wireless connection, it will do so in order to send registration data, and to connect you to the .Mac service if you signed up for it.

In this section, I'll give you the basics of how to get connected to the Internet, in both wired and wireless fashion. But presuming that the reader of this book is very likely to be a Windows user who needs to connect a Mac to network with other Macs on it, most of the ink here will be spilled in that direction.

In this section, I'm going to presume a few things about your knowledge and your situation:

- You have a high-speed, rather than a dialup, Internet connection.

- If you are working with a portable Mac, it has a built-in Wi-Fi adapter.

- You understand the basic concepts behind Internet access and simple home networking.

Let's rock 'n' roll!

Connecting to the Internet

Depending on your Internet and networking setup, getting connected can be very painless, or only slightly more complicated. Let's walk through some scenarios, from the most elemental to the relatively complex.

One Mac, connected directly to the modem

If you've got a high-speed connection through a cable or DSL modem, and your Mac is the only computer in the house, getting online is incredibly easy. You'll need an Ethernet cable, which likely came with your modem.

Here's how simple it is under this scenario to get online:

1. Follow your Internet service provider's instructions for connecting the cable or DSL modem to its network and make sure it's turned on.

2. Connect one end of the Ethernet cable to the appropriate port on your cable or DSL modem.

3. Connect the other end to the Ethernet port on your Mac.

4. Click the Safari icon 🧭 on the dock. Safari launches.

    That's it. You are now connected to the Internet.

Connecting to a hardwired router

You can think of a router as a kind of traffic cop for your Internet connection. It manages both incoming and outgoing information. And if you have multiple computers connected to the Internet via a local network, it also handles, or *routes*, data so that it gets to the right place.

There are two kinds of routers: hardwired and wireless (though almost all wireless routers also have Ethernet ports for wired connections, too). Connecting using a hardwired router is an almost identical process to plugging directly into the modem, except the router sits between the computer and the modem. You'll also need an Ethernet cable for every computer you plan to connect.

Here's the routine:

1. Connect the modem to your provider's network and make sure it's turned on.

2. Connect one end of an Ethernet cable to the wide area network (WAN) port on the back of the router, and the other end to the port on the modem.

3. Connect one end of a second cable to one of the Ethernet ports on the router, and the other end to the Ethernet port on your Mac.

4. Turn on the router and wait for it to complete its bootup process. A set of lights usually will indicate when the router is ready; check the device's manual for details.

5. Launch Safari.

   You should be connected to the Internet.

   If you have more than one computer, repeat the process until they are all connected. The process is basically the same for Windows and Mac computers. It gets a little more complicated if you're using a wireless Internet connection—but not much.

Connecting with Wi-Fi

Wi-Fi is great. It lets you create a home network without worrying about running wires. The latest version of Wi-Fi, known as 802.11n, is so fast that, under the right circumstances, it's zippier than standard Ethernet. And it also has greater range, meaning that most homes will have few, if any, dead spots.

NOTE

Apple seldom uses the term Wi-Fi in its menus and documentation. Instead it refers to its wireless system as AirPort, and calls Wi-Fi networks AirPort networks.

But there is one downside to Wi-Fi. Because it uses radio waves to connect, those signals can be intercepted. Someone sitting outside your house with a laptop can connect to a Wi-Fi network that's not secure and use it with impunity. In some cases, an evildoer could access the files on your computer, or use your Internet connection to commit a cybercrime. Or, at the very least, that irritating neighbor next door could leach off the Internet service you pay for.

This complicates connecting to the Internet, but only slightly. Mac makes even this type of connection relatively simple.

If you are setting up a wireless router in your home, you will need to read and follow the manufacturer's instructions for configuring it properly. You should set up its security using what's known as encryption. You can think of encryption as a form of data scrambling—information leaving either the computer or the router is encoded, and then decoded when it reaches its destination. A password, sometimes called an encryption key, must be employed to properly decode it.

Here's how to get online wirelessly:

 NOTE

If your AirPort card is not turned on, you can do so from Network preferences. Select the AirPort item in the left pane to see the AirPort preferences, and click the Turn Airport On button. The list of available networks should then appear. If it does not, you can click the Advanced button to manually access a list of available wireless networks.

1. Once your wireless router is properly set up, start your Macintosh if it's not already turned on. If the AirPort card in your Mac is on and active, it will recognize networks available around you, including yours, and present you with a list in a window (**FIGURE 11.7**).

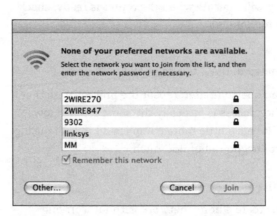

FIGURE 11.7 The Mac's AirPort adapter scans for networks and presents you with a list.

2. Select your network from the list and click the Join button. A Password field appears, along with a checked item labeled Remember This Network.

3. Enter the password that matches the one used when you set up your router (select the Show Password option if you want to see the password's characters as you type them), and click Join.

A progress meter shows the connection process, and once you're linked in, the window will close. You're now connected to the network.

You can also use this process of connecting if you're in a public Wi-Fi hotspot at a coffee shop, restaurant, hotel, or office. In those cases, you may or may not be prompted for a password. If you are, you'll have to obtain it from the operator of the network.

Connecting to a Local Area Network (LAN)

Connecting a Macintosh to a network of other Macs is a snap. Once the new Mac has joined the network, it can see all the other Macs, and they can see it. But joining a Windows network is a bit trickier. Windows PCs approach network connections a little differently. Fortunately, the Mac can adapt.

In this section, I'll presume you're adding a Mac to a Windows network, but I will provide some details on Mac-to-Mac networking.

First, though, it helps to understand some basics about networking personal computers. There are two primary aspects to networking computers:

- Getting the computers to see each other once they are all connected to the same network.

- Giving users who access networked computers permission read, write, move, and delete files.

Once connected, both Macs and Windows have a simple way to share files. A single folder, called the Public folder, can be used to share files by placing copies in them. If you don't allow access to any other folders, it acts like an airlock between machines. I leave files for you, and then you reach in and get them. You can also leave files for me, which I stop by to pick up.

However, if you'd rather not be constrained to just one folder, you can expand the number of shares. You can share folders or even whole drives. Keep in mind that you may not want to share some folders, and you probably don't want to open up your whole drive—exposing personal data and system files to anyone on your network is not always wise.

 TIP

If you travel frequently, it may help to have access to the AirPort menu from the desktop's menu bar. You can set this up in Network preferences by selecting AirPort in the left pane and then selecting the option Show Airport Status in Menu Bar. The AirPort icon 🛜 appears on the right side of the menu bar. Clicking it will give you a list of available networks, and clicking any of them will start the connection process.

 TIP

Hold down the Option key when you click the Airport icon, and then mouse over the networks in the list to see what kind of encryption they require and other information.

Configuring your network settings

In Windows networking, PCs that need to communicate with each other are given the same *workgroup name*. Computers with the same workgroup name can communicate with and share files with each other. If a computer joins a Windows network with a different workgroup name, it won't be recognized by the other computers, and it won't be able to access them.

By default, most versions of Windows use Workgroup as the default workgroup name. The exception is Windows XP Home Edition, which uses MSHome.

When you add a Mac to a Windows network, it should also be given the same workgroup name as the PCs on the LAN so that the Mac and the PCs can communicate.

Here's how to do that:

1. From System Preferences, open Network preferences.

2. Select the active connection type from the pane on the left if it's not already selected. The information to the right should change to reflect the connection you've chosen.

3. Click the Advanced button. The Advanced Network Settings dialog window appears.

4. Click the WINS tab. The WINS pane appears (**FIGURE 11.8**).

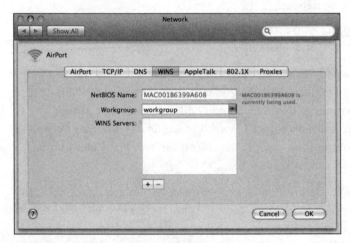

FIGURE 11.8 Use the WINS pane to give your Mac the same workgroup name as your PCs.

5. Enter the same workgroup name in the Workgroup field that you have assigned the Windows PCs on your network.

6. In the NetBIOS Name field, enter a name for your Mac to identify it on the Windows PCs.

7. Click OK. The general Network preferences pane returns.

8. Click Apply, but leave the Network preferences window open. We'll come back to it in a moment.

The first half of the process is completed. Your Mac is now on your network with a workgroup name. Now, let's set up file sharing.

Sharing folders

To begin sharing files, we'll use another preferences window—Sharing. Since we left the System Preferences up and open to Network, we'll start from there.

1. On the Network preferences window, click the Show All button. The System Preferences screen appears.

2. Click the Sharing folder. The Sharing dialog window appears (**FIGURE 11.9**).

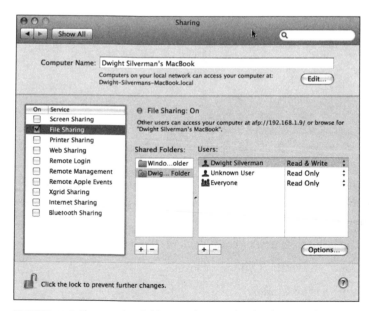

FIGURE 11.9 Choose what folders to share, and with whom, via the Sharing preferences window.

3. Select the File Sharing item in the left column. The columns on the right will change to show Shared Folders and Users.

4. Choose a folder in the Shared Folders column. The Users column will change to reflect who has what kind of access to the folder you've selected.

5. To add a folder to the Shared list, click the plus (+) sign at the bottom of the column. A Finder window appears.

6. Navigate to the folder you'd like to share, select it, and then click the Add button.

7. Choose a user from the Users list. You can click the permissions dropdown to change what each user can do with that specific folder.

8. Now click the Options button; a settings window appears (**FIGURE 11.10**). It shows the various file sharing protocols you can use, and who has access to them.

FIGURE 11.10 This window lets you enable three different types of file sharing protocols.

If you have enabled File Sharing on the previous screen, the Share Files and Folders Using AFP option should be selected by default. If it is not, select it.

9. Select the option Share Files and Folders Using SMB.

10. Click Done. The settings window closes.

11. Close the Sharing window.

You're now set up so that you can connect to a Windows network and see computers and shared drives and folders on the machines there.

To test your Mac's connectivity to the network, let's look at the Network folder on your Mac:

1. From the Finder menu bar, choose Go > Network. The Network folder opens to show the computers available on the network (**FIGURE 11.11**). Note that you can also see them under the Shared heading in the folder's sidebar on the left.

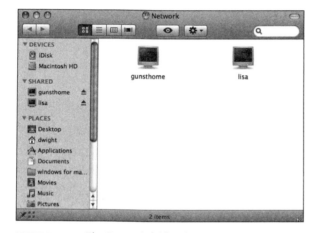

FIGURE 11.11 The Network folder shows the computers visible on your network.

2. Double-click one of the icons there, and you'll see the shared folders on that computer.

3. Is there a computer, drive or folder you'll access frequently? If so, click and drag the item under the Places heading in the sidebar. Now it'll be accessible to you from any Finder window.

Now that you know how to share folders, let's share printers.

Sharing printers

Chances are, one or more of the computers on your Windows network has a printer connected to it. You can use it from your Mac by adding it as a network printer:

1. Open System Preferences, and then click Print & Fax. The Print & Fax window opens (**FIGURE 11.12**).

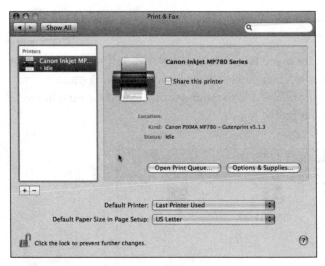

FIGURE 11.12 The Print & Fax window allows you to add and manage printers and faxes connected to your Mac, as well as across your network.

2. Click the plus sign beneath the left pane. The Add Printer window appears (**FIGURE 11.13**).

FIGURE 11.13 Add different types of printers, regardless of how they connect—USB, network, Bluetooth, and so on.

3. Click the Windows button. The window below it changes to a three-column display, with the workgroup name on the left.

4. Select the workgroup; the computers in that workgroup appear in the list.

5. Select the computer that hosts the printer you want to access. (You may be prompted for a password to access the computer, depending on how the network computer is configured.) The attached printer (or printers) appears in the right pane.

6. Select the printer you want to add.

7. Click the Print Using arrow and choose Select a Driver to Use. You'll see a list of printer drivers.

8. Scroll through the list until you see the appropriate printer driver. Select it, and then click the Add button. An Installable Options screen appears; what's on it will vary depending on the printer.

9. Make any necessary changes, and then click Continue. Both the Installable Options and Add Printer screens close, and you're back at the Print & Fax preferences page, with your new printer included in the left pane.

Want to print a test page, as you would when adding a printer in Windows? Do this:

1. In the Print & Fax preferences window, select the printer from which you want to print a test page.

2. Click the Open Print Queue button. The Print Queue window opens.

3. From the menu bar, select Printer, and then Print Test Page.

4. If you are prompted for a password to access the Windows printer, enter an appropriate password. The printer prints a test page.

5. Close the Print Queue window, and then close the Print & Fax window.

Backing Up Using Time Machine

Everyone who uses a computer knows that backing it up is a crucial part of routine maintenance. Unfortunately, for many people backing up the computer ranks right up there with getting a root canal or buying life insurance. With this in mind, Apple introduced in Leopard a new feature called Time Machine that makes backing up a truly "set it and forget it" experience.

That is, until you need it. Then, restoring is just as easy.

Time Machine works by first backing up your entire hard drive. Every hour after that, it notes changes made and backs up those changes. After 24 hours, the hourly backups are consolidated. Similar consolidations happen at the end of the week and the month.

Because the changes are noted every hour, you can "go back in time" to any specific month, week, day and hour and find a document, folder or even an entire drive and restore it.

Time Machine is designed to work primarily with an external, USB- or FireWire-based hard drive. However, it can also work with almost any hard drive connected to a Mac—internal or external. That means if you have more than one Mac using Leopard on your network, you can back up to a drive connected to that computer. Unfortunately, it cannot back up to an internal or external drive connected to a Windows computer.

I recommend buying an external drive for each Mac you have. This is the simplest and fastest way to use Time Machine, and it also gives you the most backup space. You can use a drive that's also being used for something else, but you'll have less space that you can use for backups.

Time Machine will keep saving changes to your system until the Time Machine drive is full. It will then ask you if you want to delete older changed files in order to make room for the latest ones. (It will not remove your original full backup.) You can also disconnect the full drive and connect a new one that has free space. Given that large external drives are now relatively inexpensive—500-GB drives are approaching the $100 price at this writing—replacing full Time Machine drives with new, wide-open ones is a viable option for many users.

I'm often asked how big a hard drive to use with Time Machine. My answer is usually to buy the biggest external drive you can afford. If your Mac has just one hard drive and there's plenty of available space on it, then your initial backup won't be too large. But the more software and data you add, the more space you'll need on your Time Machine drive. I like to buy an external drive that's twice as big as my Mac's primary drive—say, a 320-GB external drive to back up at 160-GB Mac hard drive.

Setting Up Time Machine

Getting Time Machine up and running is very simple. In fact, the first time you plug in an external drive you'll be asked whether it should be used for Time Machine.

Here's how Time Machine's setup works:

1. Plug in your external hard drive, or start your computer after installing a new internal drive. A dialog box appears asking if you want to use the drive to back up via Time Machine.

2. Click the Use As Backup Disk button. (If you click the Cancel button, you can still enable Time Machine later via System Preferences.) The Time Machine dialog window appears (**FIGURE 11.14**). You'll see a countdown to the starting of the initial backup.

 NOTE

In some cases, you may be prompted to erase the target hard drive, even though it's blank and there's nothing on it. That's because Time Machine requires a type of disk formatting that's different from the kind on your external drive. If you're prompted to erase the drive, select Erase. However, if there is data on it, it will be destroyed. This is another reason why it's best to dedicate a drive to Time Machine.

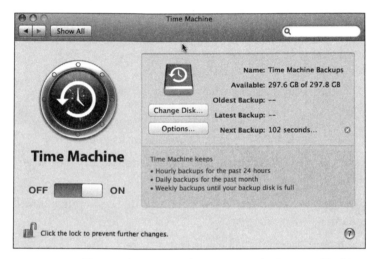

FIGURE 11.14 Time Machine counts down to its next backup—and in this case, its first backup.

3. Close the Time Machine window. Time Machine will make a complete initial backup of your hard drive. This could take quite a while, particularly on a drive with a lot of data and software.

If you chose not to immediately set up Time Machine when first prompted, you can do so from its preferences window:

1. In System Preferences, choose Time Machine. The Time Machine dialog window appears (**FIGURE 11.15**).

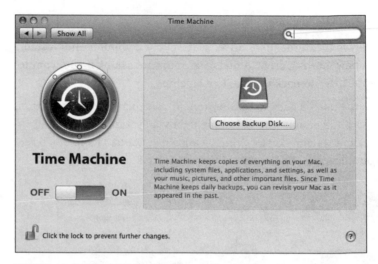

FIGURE 11.15 Turn Time Machine on or off, or select a drive to use from this screen.

2. Click Choose Backup Disk. A list of available disks appears.

3. Select the disk you want to use and click Use for Backup. The selection window closes.

4. Click the Off/On button to turn on Time Machine and initiate the backup process.

5. Close the Time Machine dialog window.

Excluding Files from Time Machine

There may be files you don't want Time Machine to back up. You can add them to an exclusion list.

1. In the Time Machine preferences window, click Options. The Do Not Back Up window appears.

2. Using the Finder, drag the files that you don't want backed up onto this window.

3. To remove an item from the list, select it and click the minus (-) button beneath the list.

4. Click Done. The list window closes.

Recovering Files with Time Machine

Recovering files with Time Machine is almost as easy as setting up the backup process. The recovery process is enhanced by a very cool 3D effect that will make you look for excuses to use it.

Let's say you want to find an older version of a word processing document you've been working on:

1. Find the current version of the file in the Finder and select it.

2. Click the Time Machine icon on the Dock, or double-click it in the Applications folder. The Mac operating system desktop slides away to reveal the Time Machine recovery interface (**FIGURE 11.16**). You'll see a space scene background, with a line of multiple Finder windows marching off into the distance—the effect is looking back in time.

   But it's more than just a pretty face. Each one of those Finder windows holds a previous version of your file.

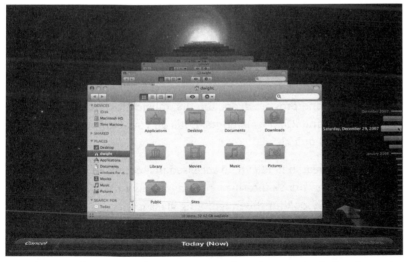

FIGURE 11.16 The Time Machine recovery interface gives you the feeling that you're looking back in time at older versions of your files.

3. There are three ways to navigate the line of folders. Choose one of the following:

   ▪ Click the pair of arrows to the right and below the first Folder windows to move back and forth in the line.

TIP

What if you want to find a file or folder that no longer exists on your Mac? You can use Spotlight, Mac's built-in search function, to locate it. Note that every Finder window you see in the line of windows in Figure 11.16 has a search field on the top right, just as every regular Finder window has. Type the name of the file you want there, and then select it from the list of search results. You'll be taken directly to the folder with the most recent version. From there you can you use the backward and forward arrow, or the tabs on the right side to find just the version you want.

- Use the notches along the right side of the screen, which are tagged by month, week, day, or time.

- Click any of the folders in the line to bring it forward.

4. Select the file in the folder you've chosen.

5. In the bar at the bottom right of the Time Machine screen, click Restore. You'll see a message that asks if you want to keep the original file, keep both the old and new files, or replace the newer file with the older one.

Keeping the original file will do nothing; the old version won't be restored. Keeping both places a copy of the older file in its original location. The current version of the file is retained, but the world "original" is added to its name. Replacing deletes the newer file and puts the older one in its place.

6. Click Close on the lower left of the Time Machine screen. Your desktop slides back into place.

Searching with Spotlight

I've touched on Spotlight here and there throughout this book. It's a fast, effective way to find things on your Mac. If you use Windows Vista and its new, improved search function, you'll find Spotlight to be very similar. It can find programs, documents, music files, video, calendar items, e-mail, and iChat transcripts. If it's on your computer, Spotlight will find it, and quickly.

The Spotlight search field can be accessed in a couple of places in the Mac operating system's interface, making it easy to access whenever you need it. Just look for the magnifying glass icon.

To find Spotlight's search field, click the Spotlight icon 🔍 on the far right of the menu bar. The search field appears just below the icon (**FIGURE 11.17**).

FIGURE 11.17 Spotlight's search field appears when you click the magnifying glass icon on the menu bar.

You can also find the search field on the top right of every Finder window (**FIGURE 11.18**).

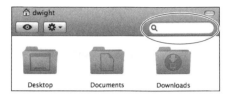

FIGURE 11.18 Every Finder window has a Spotlight search field. Handy!

Using these two methods yields the same results, but they are displayed in different ways.

Searching via the Menu bar

When you use Spotlight on the menu bar, you'll see results displayed in a dropdown menu. To search from the menu bar:

1. Click the Spotlight icon. The Spotlight search field appears.

2. Enter your search term or terms. As you type, Spotlight begins to show results based on the letters you've typed so far. When typing is complete, Spotlight displays results by category in a dropdown list (**FIGURE 11.19**).

FIGURE 11.19 Spotlight displays results from the menu bar field in a list, sorted by category.

The results in Figure 11.19 show many "hits" on the word *sprint*, the first being the definition from the Mac operating system's built-in dictionary.

TIP

Note how fast the results come up. That speed, combined with your pressing Enter to launch the first item on the list, turn Spotlight into a command-line program launcher. For example, if you want to launch Excel for the Mac, but don't want to hunt it down in the Applications folder, you can simply type *Excel*, press Enter and the spreadsheet program launches. If you're a fast typist, this can get you going quicker than using a mouse to launch programs.

3. Click any of the items on the list to launch it in its associated program.

   or

   Press the Enter key to launch the very first item on the list.

Searching Via the Finder Window

In the section in this chapter on Time Machine, I mentioned using Spotlight to find files that had been backed up. To do that, you use the Spotlight field in the Finder window.

The field works the same way as the menu bar version, but with one difference: The results are displayed in a Finder window, and you have some additional options for refining your search once the results are complete.

To use Spotlight in a Finder window:

1. From any Finder window (I'm using the Home folder, labeled Dwight in this example), enter your search term or terms in the Spotlight field in the upper right. As you type, the results fill in and the folder takes on some additional features (**FIGURE 11.20**).

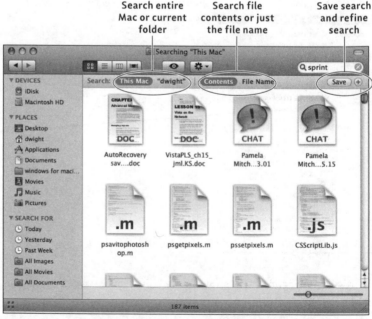

FIGURE 11.20 The Finder window's Spotlight results are shown in whatever view you've set for the Finder—Icons (shown), List, Column, or Cover Flow.

At first, the results are the same as the ones you'd get searching from the menu bar, and they come from any folder on your hard drive. But there are some new buttons across the top of the results window that let you focus the results. In the Search category, for example, you'll see This Mac selected.

2. Select the folder name—in this case, I am selecting Dwight, my Home folder—to see results in only that folder.

3. By default, the search includes the word found in the contents of any document. Click File Name to search for only the names of files.

4. To further refine the search, click the plus button at the far right of the window. You'll get a second level of buttons and dropdowns that let you apply filters to the search. Each level includes a plus and minus button, which adds more complexity to the search.

5. Click the Save button to save the search as you've crafted it. A dialog box appears.

6. Name the search; by default it's saved to the Saved Searches folder. A checkbox in the dialog window lets you add the search to the Search For category in the Finder sidebar. If you do this, the saved search will show up in every Finder sidebar.

7. Click the Save button to save the search. The Save dialog window closes.

8. Close the Finder window.

 TIP

You can control which categories show up first in a Spotlight search via the Spotlight window in System Preferences. Just drag the items in the Search Results list in the order you prefer.

Organizing with Spaces

Spaces is the Mac operating system's new virtual desktop manager. It allows you to have multiple Mac desktops and, if you are using Parallels Desktop for Mac or VMware Fusion, a full-screen Windows desktop as well. I showed you how to set up Windows in a Spaces desktop in "Giving Windows its very own Space" in Chapter 4.

This section focuses on configuring Spaces for a different task: organizing your running programs. You can set up Spaces so that programs launch on specific desktops. This is particularly handy on a notebook computer with limited screen real estate, because you can assign programs to their own desktops where they'll have more breathing room.

In this section, I'm assuming you already have Spaces enabled—see Chapter 4 if you don't—and that the Spaces icon is on your Dock.

Assigning Programs to Spaces Desktops

Let's say you're working in Microsoft Word, but you also need to edit images for use in the document in Adobe Photoshop. As you'll recall from Chapter 4, each desktop in Spaces is assigned a number, and you can have Word active on Desktop 1 and Photoshop on Desktop 2. But even cooler: You can set up Spaces so that Photoshop always launches in Desktop 2! Then you don't have to launch the program and manually move it.

Here's how to assign programs to launch in specific Spaces desktops:

1. From System Preferences, click Exposé & Spaces and then click the Spaces button at the top of the Exposé & Spaces window.

   or

   Right-click or Command-click the Spaces icon in the Dock and choose Spaces Preferences from the menu that appears. The Spaces pane displays (**FIGURE 11.21**). The Application Assignments area in the middle of the window is where we'll be working.

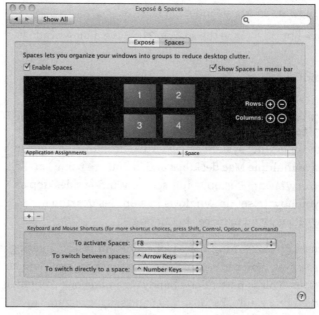

FIGURE 11.21 The Spaces pane lets you assign applications to desktops, and create additional desktops if you need them.

2. Click the plus button on the left below the Applicant Assignments field. A Finder window opens showing the contents of the Applications folder.

3. Find and select the application you'd like to assign, and then click Add. The Finder window closes and the program appears in the Application Assignments field with a desktop assigned to it. In most cases, this will be Desktop 1 (**FIGURE 11.22**).

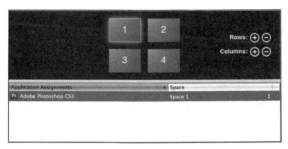

FIGURE 11.22 In the Applications Assignments field, choose the Spaces desktop in which you'd like the program to always launch.

In the Spaces grid above it, which shows your available desktops, the active desktop is highlighted.

4. In the Application Assignment field, click the name of the currently assigned Space. A menu appears, showing all the available Spaces desktop.

5. Choose the desktop to which you're assigning the program. The grid highlight above the Application Assignments field changes to indicate your new choice.

6. Close the Exposé & Spaces dialog window.

Now, each time you launch the application, it will start up in the assigned Spaces desktop. Use the Spaces icon and the full-screen grid described in Chapter 4 to access it. You can also get to individual desktops by holding down the Control key and keying in the number of the Spaces desktop; for example, press Control + 1, 2, or 3.

Adding or Removing Spaces Desktops

If you're a serious multitasker, you may want to have more than the four default Spaces desktops. You can add more desktops two at a time—up to 16—and you can also remove them.

To add or remove Spaces desktops:

1. In the Spaces pane of the Exposé & Spaces dialog window (Figure 11.21), note the default set of four desktops represented in the grid, along with a series of plus and minus icons next to the Rows and Columns labels.

2. Click the plus icon next to Rows to add an additional two more Spaces desktops. They appear at the bottom of the grid, numbered 5 and 6. To remove them, click the minus icon for Rows.

3. Click the plus icon next to the columns to add more Spaces desktops to the right of the grid. Two more will be added in a vertical column, and this will change your numbering layout. In the default layout, Desktops 1 and 2 are located at the top, and Desktops 3 and 4 are at the bottom. Now, Desktops 1, 2, and 3 are at the top, and 4, 5, and 6 are at the bottom (**FIGURE 11.23**).

FIGURE 11.23 When you add columns of additional desktops, it changes the layout.

To remove a column, click the Columns minus icon.

4. Close the Spaces window.

Staying Secure

Listen up, Windows users!

Some of you have made the leap to a Macintosh because you're tired and frustrated with dealing with Windows' security issues. Users of Microsoft's operating system feel constantly bombarded with viruses, spyware, hacking, and phishing attempts. Apple has touted the Mac as being a haven from these woes, and longtime Mac aficionados will swear that you simply don't have to worry about these issues if you'll just follow the Right Path.

So is this true? Are you immune from the security assaults that are associated with Windows?

It's true that, historically, the Mac OS X has not had the same kinds of problems as Windows. But that doesn't mean Macs won't be immune in the future.

Some security experts point to the fact that today's writers of viruses and spyware are motivated by money, not notoriety. In the past, evil-doers were happy to trash computers en masse just for the bragging rights. But today malicious software is often used to spread spam or steal private information, all with the goal of making an illicit profit. And, as the Mac becomes more popular, it will become a bigger target for those seeking to take advantage of a growing pool of users.

This means that, if you're a Windows user seeking refuge in the Mac, you'd still be smart not to let your guard down. Consider these facts:

- 2007 saw the first spyware attack aimed directly at the Mac operating system. It attempted to lure Mac users into downloading what was allegedly a file needed to view video. Instead, users are tricked into installing a program that redirects their Web browsers to sites with malicious intent.

- No software is bug-free, and that includes the Mac. ZDNet's George Ou reported that, in 2007, Apple issued patches fixing 243 security-related bugs, 234 of which were rated as Highly Critical by Secunia, a noted security consulting firm. By contrast, Microsoft fixed 44 security-related bugs in Windows XP and Vista combined, 27 of which were rated as Extremely or Highly Critical. (The Mac operating system had no Extremely Critical flaws, based on Secunia's rating system.)

- Many Macintosh users don't use antivirus or anti-malware programs, even though security experts recommend they do. This means that if a virulent virus, Trojan or worm infection hits the Mac community, it could spread very quickly—there's a lot of fresh kindling out there to feed a fire.

- Finally, many Windows users who are moving to the Mac to get away from spyware and viruses may bring their bad habits with them. In many cases, Windows users bring security issues upon themselves. A major aspect of getting malware onto a user's computer is a process known as "social engineering," a fancy phrase for trickery. Just because someone is using a Mac doesn't mean they are less prone to being fooled.

With those points in mind, let's look at some things you can do to keep your Mac safe.

Stay Up to Date

Just as with Windows, it's important to keep your Mac's software up to date. The Software Update application does this automatically, on a weekly basis. Apple releases patches for security issues more quickly than Microsoft, which waits until the second Tuesday of every month to issue fixes. In the Software Update window in System Preferences, you can change that to daily or monthly. I'd recommend daily.

Stay Alert

Just as you would when working in Windows, practice safe software. Don't click attachments or unfamiliar Web links you receive in e-mails you weren't expecting. Avoid locations that are common lures for those attempting to place malware on computers, such as porn or online gambling sites. Don't give your passwords to anyone who asks for it. And make sure your Mac login is password protected, which you can do from the Accounts window in System Preferences.

Shed Your Administrator Hat

It's a good idea not to use an administrator level account day to day with your Mac. You can create a Standard account whose activities won't affect other users on your computer in Accounts preferences. If you have children who use your Mac, set up Managed With Parental Controls accounts for them, which blocks potentially dangerous tasks such as installing software, also done through Accounts preferences.

To create a new account:

1. In System Preferences, click Accounts. The Accounts preferences window opens (**FIGURE 11.24**).

2. Click the lock at the bottom of the left pane. You'll be prompted for an administrator password; enter it and click OK. The lock will swing open with a click.

3. Click the plus icon above the lock. The New Account window appears.

4. Click the New Account dropdown arrows; the menu appears.

5. Depending on which account you'd like to create, select either Standard or Managed with Parental Controls.

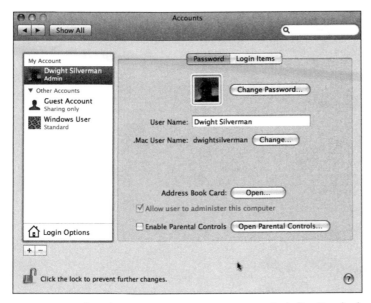

FIGURE 11.24 From here you can create new accounts, including Standard and Managed with Parental Controls.

6. Fill in the rest of the form with your login name, a short name (nickname), password, and a password hint, if necessary.

7. Click Create Account. The New Account window closes, and the Account preferences window for your new account displays. If you selected a Managed with Parental Controls account, this item on the window will be selected. If you selected a Standard Account, it will be deselected, and you can select it to enable Parental Controls.

8. Make any necessary changes to the settings, and then close the Accounts window.

Turn on Your Firewall

Finally, but most importantly, you should turn on the Mac's firewall, which by default in Leopard is effectively disabled. The firewall keeps unwanted, potentially malicious external connections from being made to your Mac, so you'll want to turn it on, and here's how:

1. In System Preferences, click Security. The Security preferences window appears.

2. Click the Firewall button. The Firewall pane appears (**FIGURE 11.25**). Note that Allow All Incoming Connections is already selected, which leaves your Mac wide open.

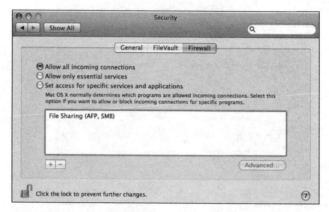

FIGURE 11.25 The firewall settings let you configure the Mac's firewall in three ways.

Note that you have two other choices:

- **Allow Only Essential Services** lets outside computers connect to components of the operating system that require access. For example, iChat may need to communicate with other computers to conduct a video chat session. This would be considered an essential service.

- **Set Access for Specific Services and Applications** lets you control which programs and services can receive incoming connections. If you have turned on certain features using the Sharing preferences, such as file or printer sharing, those services will automatically be added here.

In most cases, the middle option, Allow Only Essential Services, will provide a good balance of protection and convenience.

3. Select Allow Only Essential Services.

4. Close the Security window if you are finished.

If you're truly concerned about security, you alternatively can select the third option and manually add the programs and services that you want to receive connections, or designate a program that you always want to be blocked.

To manually add a program to the allow-or-block list:

1. In the Firewall preferences pane, select Set Access for Specific Services and Applications.

2. Click the plus icon below the applications list field. A Finder window for the Applications folder appears.

3. Select the program you would like to block or allow, and then click Add. The program appears in the application list, with Allow Incoming Connections showing as the default setting to the right of the program's name.

4. To block the program, click the arrows to the right of Allow Incoming Connections, and then select Block Incoming Connections from the dropdown menu that appears.

5. Close the Security preferences window when you're finished.

Get Stealthy

Want an extra layer of protection? You can set the Mac's firewall so that it will not allow responses when probed by external programs, such as pings.

1. In the Firewall pane of the Security preferences window, make sure either Allow Only Essential Services or Set Access for Specific Services and Applications is selected, and then click the Advanced button below the applications list. A dialog box appears.

2. Click the box next to Enable Stealth Mode and click OK.

3. Close the Security preferences window.

Now that you know about the Mac operating system's advanced features, let's move on to an overview of some of the applications that come with the Mac.

chapter 12

Mac Apps:
An Overview

I once heard an operating system described as "the computer's underwear"—the stuff you don't see under the spiffy outer threads, but that, in its own way, is just as important.

Modern operating systems are both the underwear and the stylish new suit or dress. This is certainly true for Mac OS X, which comes with a slew of free programs. And when you buy a Mac, Apple throws in a suite of consumer applications called iLife that extend your computer's capabilities even further.

In this chapter, I'll provide an overview of the most-used applications that come with the Mac operating system, including a brief look at the stars of the iLife suite. You'll learn what each does, where it's found, and whether it has a Windows counterpart.

For more detailed information, I again recommend Robin Williams' *Mac OS X 10.5 Leopard: Peachpit Learning Series*.

Surfin' with Safari

Safari is the Web browser that's included with the Mac, the counterpart to Internet Explorer in Windows (**FIGURE 12.1**). For Windows users who are curious about how Safari works, there's a version available for that operating system at www.apple.com/safari.

FIGURE 12.1 Safari is Apple's Web browser, and the latest version includes some nifty new features.

By default, Safari sits on the Mac's Dock, and also is accessible via the Applications folder. It's version 3.0 of Apple's browser, and it has some unique features:

- **Private browsing** lets you surf Web pages without leaving tracks. No information is saved between sessions—history, cookies, auto-fill of forms, and so on. When you close the browser, all traces of your steps are removed.

- **Tabbed browsing** is available, just as it is in Internet Explorer 7 and Firefox in Windows, but with a twist: If you want to convert a tab to its own separate browser window, just drag the tab to the desktop.

- **An RSS feed reader** is built-in, as it is in Firefox and IE7.

- **SnapBack** lets you quickly return to a specific page. Mark any page as a SnapBack, and jump to it quickly from any other page.

Safari has a clean, Spartan design that some Windows users may find, well, a bit *too* Spartan. For example, there isn't even a home page button on Safari's toolbar. You can add it, though, by customizing the toolbar:

1. Right-click Safari's toolbar and from the menu that appears, choose Customize Toolbar. A window with available icons appears.

2. Click an icon you'd like to add—say, the house icon, which calls up your brower's home page—and drag it into position on the toolbar.

3. Click the Done button when you're finished customizing the toolbar.

Want alternatives? Windows users who like Mozilla's Firefox browser will be happy to know there's a version of it for the Mac, available at www.firefox.com. But you may also want to try a browser that's smaller, takes fewer system resources, and has a more "Mac-like" interface. Camino uses the same software engine for rendering Web pages as Firefox, but it's faster and has a simpler toolbar. Get it at www.caminobrowser.org.

Connecting with iChat

On one level, the Mac's iChat application is an instant messaging (IM) client, but unlike Windows Messenger, you can talk to more than just one IM network. iChat works with AOL's AIM; Apple's .Mac; Jabber, an open-source instant messaging platform; Gtalk, Google's IM service (which uses Jabber); and Bonjour, a networking protocol created by Apple. You can have multiple accounts running at once, either in separate windows or consolidated into one with tabs representing each chat.

But iChat can do much more than that. It makes video conferencing a breeze, even with more than one person at a time. If you and other participants all have Leopard, you can also share documents and photos during a video chat with a feature called iChat Theater (**FIGURE 12.2**). iChat can even allows you to control the screen of another iChat user via screen sharing.

FIGURE 12.2 If all parties are using Leopard, you can share photos and documents while video chatting in iChat.

iChat even comes to your rescue when your surroundings are, um, less than attractive. It can present a different background during a video chat, including animated ones. Want it to look like you're chatting from the front car of a roller coaster? Try this:

1. In the iChat menu bar, select Video, and then Video Preview. The Video Preview window opens, showing your smiling face.

2. Once again, from the menu, choose Video > Video Effects. The Video Effects window opens.

3. Click the directional arrows at the bottom left or right to page through the various effects until you come to the roller coaster background (usually page 3).

4. Select the roller coaster background. A message asks you to "Please step out of the frame."

5. Move away from the camera until you are no longer visible in the preview window. After a few seconds, the animated background appears in the Preview Window.

6. Sit back down in front of the computer and click the camera icon next to a video-enabled person on your buddy list. A larger video window appears with a notice at the top indicating you've asked for a video chat.

When the other person accepts, the video window showing your image shrinks, while the other person's grows to fill most of the screen. Your smaller preview shows your face and background as the other person sees it (**FIGURE 12.3**).

FIGURE 12.3 Your video preview, lower right, shows your face and background as your video-enabled buddy sees it.

7. To restore the original background, from the menu bar choose Video > Show Video Effects. The original background is in the center of each page in the Video Effects window.

iChat is powerful and friendly enough that you may not want alternatives, but there are plenty out there. If you miss chatting with your MSN Messenger friends, try Adium at www.adiumx.com, which supports MSN and a slew of other IM services, including Yahoo! and ICQ. However, Adium does not support voice or video chats.

In addition, Apple offers a version of Messenger for Mac at www.apple.com/downloads/macosx/email_chat/messengerformac.html. It also does not support video or audio chats at this writing.

You've Got Mail

The Mac operating system's e-mail application is called, appropriately enough, Mail (**FIGURE 12.4**). It's joined at the hip by the Address Book, which stores your contact and e-mail recipient information, similar to the setup found in Windows Mail for Windows Vista and in Outlook Express for Windows XP.

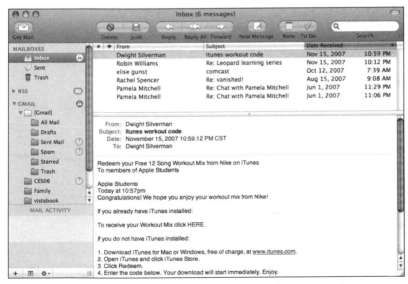

FIGURE 12.4 The Mac's Mail application does a lot more than just e-mail.

In some ways, Apple Mail is closer in capabilities to Microsoft's flagship e-mail application, Outlook. It includes a to-do list, a built-in notepad, fancy HTML-based stationary, and something called Data Detectors, which can spot addresses, dates, and phone numbers in an e-mail and respond accordingly.

Data Detectors places a dropdown menu of choices next to information it can act on. For example, it can spot contact information in an e-mail signature, with the dropdown menu that gives you the option of automatically generating an entry in the Address Book.

Mail also sports a dramatically simplified way of setting up new accounts. It auto-senses the most common types of e-mail accounts—Google's Gmail, AOL and Yahoo!—as well as standard POP3 and IMAP accounts. Setting up a new account is, in most cases, a matter of filling in your e-mail address and password and clicking the Continue button. It will not connect to a Microsoft Exchange server, however, unless the server has the IMAP protocol enabled.

Mail can also be used to read RSS feeds. Yes, you can do that in Safari, but having RSS feeds in the same application as e-mail is convenient and makes sense. By default, Safari is the Mac's default RSS reader, but you can make Mail the default reader:

1. With Mail open, click Mail in the menu bar, and then Preferences. The Mail Preferences window opens.

2. Select the RSS icon. The RSS preferences window appears.

3. Click the Default RSS Reader dropdown menu and choose Mail.

4. Close the Mail Preferences window.

5. Click an RSS link in any browser. Mail opens with a dialog box and the link you clicked highlighted.

6. Click the Add button to add the RSS feed to Mail.

You may now read the feed in the left sidebar in Mail.

Plan It with iCal

Apple's calendar application takes a step closer to becoming a serious business planning tool with the Leopard version of iCal. It's fast, tightly integrated with Mail and the Address Book, and lets multiple users access group calendars and events. But it's still very simple to use, sporting a clean, streamlined new interface (**FIGURE 12.5**).

FIGURE 12.5 Don't let iCal's simple looks fool you. There's power underneath that sleek skin.

For example, Data Detectors in Mail can spot dates—even extrapolating the next day's date and time from phrases such as "tomorrow at noon"—and add them as events in iCal.

iCal, which is similar to Windows Calendar in Windows Vista, takes a step closer to competing with Outlook's powerful calendar features. It can work with a CalDAV server, which uses a proposed, standards-based calendaring protocol, to allow delegation, create group meetings, even reserve meeting rooms.

But you don't need a server if users are sharing a Mac. Members of a family, for example, can each create his or her own calendars and share them with each other. And if you have a .Mac account, you can publish your calendar on the Internet for even non-Mac users to see.

Rockin' with iTunes

If you've got an iPod, then you already know about iTunes, even if you're a Windows user. It's the software used to manage digital music and video, synchronize your media collection with the iPod or iPhone, and make video and music purchases from the iTunes Store.

The interface is almost identical in both the Windows and Macintosh versions (**FIGURE 12.6**). The mostly minor differences are found in the menus of the two versions, to comply with standard layout conventions for Windows and Mac menus.

FIGURE 12.6 Fortunately for Windows users who switch to the Mac, iTunes is basically the same on both platforms.

If you're a Windows user switching to the Mac, and if you don't have an iPod, you'll find that iTunes serves the same purpose as Windows Media Player. However, you'll also discover that iTunes can't play any WMA media files with copy protection that you may have acquired through Windows. In fact, if you have ripped songs from CDs to unprotected WMA files using Windows Media Player, you'll find that iTunes can't play those, either.

Microsoft makes a version of Windows Media Player for Mac, but it is fairly old and has not been updated in several years. For playing unprotected WMA files, your best bet is to download a free plug-in for QuickTime called Windows Media Components, available at the following URL: www.microsoft.com/windows/windowsmedia/player/wmcomponents.mspx.

It won't help with copy-protected files, though. The best thing to do is burn them to a CD, then rip the songs to unprotected digital media files using the Mac version of iTunes.

By default, iTunes rips songs from CDs in unprotected Advanced Audio Coding (AAC) format. However, you can change this and use other formats, including MP3s, which can be played on almost any device. To change the format in the Mac or Windows version:

1. Open iTunes on the Mac, and from the iTunes menu bar, choose iTunes > Preferences.

   or

   Open iTunes in Windows, and from the iTunes menu bar, choose Edit > Preferences.

   The iTunes Preferences window appears.

2. Select Advanced, and then Importing. The Importing preferences window appears.

3. Select the Import Using dropdown and choose from one of five options: AAC, AIFF, Apple Lossless, MP3, and WAV. For the purposes of this exercise, choose MP3.

4. Select the Settings dropdown and choose a bit rate. The higher the bit rate, the better the file will sound. But be aware that higher bit rates also produce larger files. 192 kbps is a good compromise between quality and file size, so for this exercise, choose that option.

5. Click OK to close the Preferences window.

Now, songs you rip from CDs will be saved in the standard MP3 format, which can be played on any device, including an iPod.

Digging Dashboard

Dashboard is a collection of small programs that display very specific bits of information. It's similar to the Sidebar in Windows Vista, though unlike the Sidebar, Dashboard is hidden from view until you invoke it with a keystroke.

Its applets, called widgets, provide information such as weather, stock prices, date and time, system information, and so on. There are literally hundreds of other widgets you can download from www.apple.com/downloads/dashboard.

How Dashboard is invoked depends on your Mac. On a MacBook, for example, just pressing the F12 key will bring it forward. In an aluminum iMac, Function + F12 does the trick (**FIGURE 12.7**). You can also invoke it from the Dashboard icon ⚫ in the Applications folder.

FIGURE 12.7 Dashboard is a quick way to get specific, timely information onto your desktop.

Dashboard has been around for a while in the Mac, but in Leopard, Apple added the ability for you to make your own widgets from any Web page. Safari includes the ability to select an area from a page and save it as a Dashboard widget. The next time you invoke Dashboard, the area of the page you selected is updated and displayed. Here's how to create what Apple calls a Web Clip:

1. In Safari, navigate to a page you'd like to turn into a Dashboard widget.

2. Click the Web Clip icon 🔲 in the Safari toolbar. The Web page grays out.

3. Move your cursor over the area you'd like to turn into a Web Clip. Safari guesses the area and highlights it. You can adjust the size of the box, but in most cases, Safari will accurately highlight what you want capture.

4. Click the Add button in the upper right of the Safari window. Dashboard is invoked, and your Web clip is now visible.

5. Move your cursor to the lower right of the Web Clip and click the small i to bring up a menu that lets you change the border and resize the frame.

6. Click Done when you've finished editing your Web Clip.

Get an iLife

When you buy a Macintosh, Apple includes a suite of programs dubbed iLife. These five programs aren't necessarily part of the Mac operating system—and, in fact, Apple also sells the suite separately for $80—but their presence provides a lot of value. They're consumer-level applications, but in some cases they are powerful enough to handle professional work.

The latest version at this writing is iLife '08, introduced in mid-2007. It comes with iPhoto, for managing and editing digital images; GarageBand, for creating music; iMovie, for editing video; iDVD, for turning your edited video into DVDs; and iWeb, a Web site editor. By default, the programs' icons appear in the Dock, and they can also be found in the Applications folder.

I'll provide a quick overview of each of the five applications here. For a detailed look at the programs, check out Jim Heid's *The Macintosh iLife 08* (Peachpit Press, 2008).

iPhoto

Chances are good iPhoto is the program you'll use the most in the iLife suite, since most folks now use a digital camera for their photos. iPhoto, which is similar to Windows Vista's Photo Gallery, is designed to make it easy to move images from your camera onto your Mac, organize them, and do basic editing (**FIGURE 12.8**).

The latest version also lets you create Web albums that can be posted online if you also have a .Mac account. In a feature called photocasting, friends who are also .Mac users can subscribe to your photo albums, which are imported into their copies of iPhoto. When you update iPhoto and your Web albums, the photos are added to your friends' computers via .Mac. In addition, other iPhoto/.Mac users can, if you allow it, upload photos to your gallery.

FIGURE 12.8 Apply effects and do other editing tasks with the latest version of iPhoto.

The newest version also stores photos based on Events. When you first import images into iPhoto from your camera, photos are grouped into Events based on dates. In the Event view, you see a single representative thumbnail, even though an Event may have hundreds of photos. You can drag an Event and drop it onto another one, consolidating them and making it easier to organize large numbers of photos.

GarageBand

For those who love music—and especially creating it—GarageBand is a killer app for the Macintosh. In fact, I know several former Windows users who got a Mac just so they could get their hands on GarageBand.

GarageBand lets you create songs by stitching together bits of music, called Loops, played by a wide variety of instruments. Building tunes is a simple matter of dragging and dropping the instruments and styles you want into place and tweaking their sound.

Simple as it is, GarageBand is also very powerful, and it's used by professional musicians as well. In fact, some musicians, such as the rock band Nine Inch Nails, release versions of their songs in GarageBand format and allow fans to remix the tracks (**FIGURE 12.9**).

FIGURE 12.9 GarageBand lets you create your own music, or remix songs by others.

The newest version ads a feature aimed at total nonmusicians. Magic GarageBand plays a series of songs in certain genres—rock, roots rock, funk, reggae, country, and so on—and then allows you to substitute instruments to change the sound of the songs. A clever interface displays the instruments on a stage, and a Your Instrument feature lets you play along (**FIGURE 12.10**). The resulting mix can be saved as a GarageBand file and edited in the main interface.

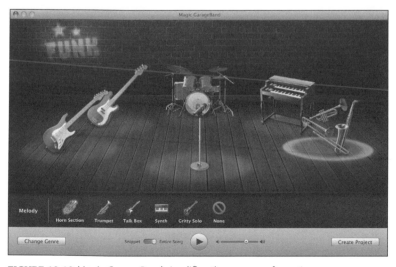

FIGURE 12.10 Magic GarageBand simplifies the process of creating your own songs.

iMovie

iMovie, the equivalent to Movie Maker in Windows, is used for editing video, as well as keeping your video collection organized. It can handle many different video formats, including high-definition ones, and can get video from many sources, including hard drives, memory-based cameras and traditional tape-based cameras.

As with iPhoto, iMovie organizes your videos based on events, which you can drag and drop to consolidate as needed. Editing video is also very simple—just drag clips into place to assemble a video project (**FIGURE 12.11**).

FIGURE 12.11 Combine video clips, and then drag them into the desired order to build your iMovie project.

iMovie's editing tools make it easy to find just the scene you're after. You can skim through the frames in a clip just by dragging your mouse across the clip's thumbnail; as you do, the clips contents play in a viewer in iMovie. Once you find what you want, you can highlight the frames and drag them into your project.

The latest version also lets you upload a video you've edited directly to YouTube, or send it to Apple TV, an iPhone, or an iPod.

iDVD

In a sense, iDVD, similar to Windows DVD Maker, is what ties iPhoto, iMovie, iTunes, and GarageBand together. You can use the program to create DVDs that will work in any DVD player, filled with your movies, music, and stills (**FIGURE 12.12**).

FIGURE 12.12 iDVD lets you compile movies, music, and picture slideshows into slick DVDs, complete with animated menus.

The program comes with dozens of themes that automate the process of building the slick menus you see at the start of professionally produced DVDs. If you include movies, for example, you'll see animated thumbnails of their content playing as part of the menu. You can choose from songs in iTunes or created with GarageBand to play as background music while the menu is on the screen.

If you'd rather build your own menu, iDVD comes with a library of buttons and tools to alter the layout of existing themes. When you're finished, you can burn up to two hours of content onto a DVD. A new Professional Quality setting gives you the best possible look, though iDVD won't burn to Blu-Ray or HD-DVD disks.

iWeb

If you ever wanted to have your own Web site, but blogs seem too geeky and building one is too intimidating, iWeb is for you. There's only one catch: If you don't have a .Mac account, getting the site you built via iWeb won't be nearly as easy.

iWeb lets you choose from a series of professionally designed page templates, which you can then tweak to suit your tastes (**FIGURE 12.13**). Adding photos is a snap: Just drag where you see existing placeholder images, and edit them in place if needed.

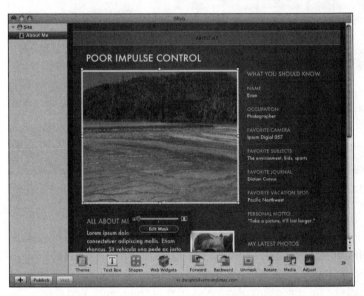

FIGURE 12.13 iWeb lets you start building your Web page with themed templates, which you then customize to make them your own.

But the pages you build with iWeb don't have to be just text and pictures. The newest version lets you add Web widgets—small applications that provide information, similar to the ones found in Dashboard. You can use Web Widgets to paste in stock information, videos, news tickers, and more. You can also insert videos and music found on your Mac's hard drive.

When you're ready to post it to the Web, you can do so through your .Mac account. If you don't have an account, you can save the pages, images, and other components to a folder. You'll then need a Web-hosting service capable of handling the site you've built.

part III

Windows for Macintosh Users

chapter 13

Windows Basics

Many Mac users approach using Windows with trepidation, particularly if they've never actually spent any quality time with Microsoft's operating system. They've heard Windows is just a cheap copy of the Mac, that viruses and malware lurk around every bend, and that it crashes hourly, and must be reinstalled weekly.

But you know what? Once they get to using it, those anxieties melt away. Don't tell anyone, but get this: Some of 'em actually *like* it!

Windows is similar enough to the Mac that the learning curve is not too steep. The most recent versions of Windows, XP and Vista, are actually quite stable, as long as they're properly maintained. If you're a Mac user who needs to run Windows because you want to use a particular piece of software, be compatible with a client, or play Windows games, you'll find the experience a mostly painless one—so long as you compute smartly.

Be Smart and Master the Basics

It's very true that Windows is a huge target for the community of malware writers and hackers. But as I wrote in the section on Mac security in Chapter 11, user behavior is a major reason why Windows systems become infected with malicious software.

In this chapter, I'll talk about the basics you need to navigate Windows. You'll learn about the desktop, Start menu and the taskbar, of which the latter two are the equivalent of the Dock and Finder on the Mac. I'll also tell you where to find your programs and documents, and how to work with folders in Windows. In the next chapter, I provide tips for staying safe.

But first things first. Let's look at the differences between using the keyboard and, particularly, the mouse in Windows versus the Mac.

Getting It Right with the Mouse

Although Apple's use of a mouse predates that of Microsoft's—text-based MS-DOS was all the rage when the Mac was introduced in 1984—Windows' navigation actually presumes more reliance on the mouse than the Mac. That's because, for years, Apple sold Macs with a one-button mouse, requiring users to hold down a modifier key, such as Command or Control, when clicking to invoke a menu or command.

But once Windows hit the scene, PCs almost always came with a mouse that had at least two buttons. Apple now sells its Macs with the Mighty Mouse, which has multiple buttons, but many longtime Mac users remain in the habit of using modifier keys.

If you are a Mac user who needs to run Windows, you'll need to break that one-button habit and get used to using the right mouse button. Trust me, it's the right (pun very much intended) thing to do.

If you're not used to using the right mouse button on a Mac, spend some time just clicking around with it in Windows: Right-click icons, window backgrounds, the taskbar, the Start button, and so on. Almost any object in Windows has some kind of context menu that appears with a right-click (and this is also true of the Mac).

To illustrate, let's practice on the desktop while at the same time possibly customizing some of your desktop's look and feel:

1. Right-click the open Windows desktop. A context menu appears.

2. Select Personalize. The Personalization menu appears (**FIGURE 13.1**). For this exercise, let's change the background, also known as wallpaper in Windows.

3. Select Desktop Background. The Choose a Desktop Background window appears, with a selection of wallpaper images within a scrollable menu. Normally, you'd just click one of these and it would become your desktop's background, but here's where we're headed right!

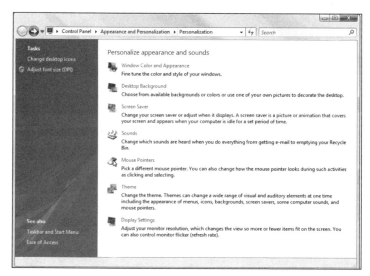

FIGURE 13.1 The Personalization menu, accessed by right-clicking the desktop, lets you customize Windows Vista to your liking.

4. Right-click the wallpaper image you think you might like to use. The image becomes your background, but also, a context menu appears (**FIGURE 13.2**). The menu lets you preview, print, or open the background image in a picture-editing program, along with other options.

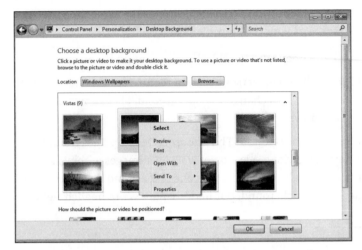

FIGURE 13.2 Right-click context menus are everywhere in Windows, even on wallpaper thumbnails.

5. Select Preview to see a larger version of the image. The Preview window opens with the image.

6. Right-click the image to get to yet another context menu.

   So you get the point, right? Context menus are everywhere in Windows. Get used to using them, and they'll be your best friends.

7. Click the red X in the right-hand corner of each of the windows you've opened in this exercise to close them.

What About Windows Keyboards?

In Chapter 9, I looked at both mice and keyboards on the Mac. Given that you're probably running Windows on a Mac if you bought this book, and that you've most likely already noticed the key-combo equivalents table in Chapter 9, there's no need for a separate section on Windows keyboards in this chapter.

However, on the chance you decide to buy a Windows keyboard to go with your Mac, there's one key you'll want to be aware of: The Windows key. On most Windows keyboards, it has the Windows logo ⊞ on it, and is located in the lower left-hand corner of the keyboard.

continues on next page

continued from previous page

What About Windows Keyboards?

Pressing the Windows key by itself opens the Start menu, which I'll detail later in the chapter. Holding down the Windows key and pressing the Tab button invokes Flip 3D, a cool way to navigate programs in Windows Vista, which I'll also talk about later.

There's no standard Windows keyboard layout. Multimedia keys, program launching keys, even some function keys may be in different locations on keyboards made by different companies—even on keyboards made by the same company! But nearly all USB-based Windows keyboards will work when plugged into the Mac, and some may come with drivers that enable special capabilities on a Mac. Check with the keyboard's documentation to learn more.

The Basics of the Windows Desktop

Just as on the Mac, a virgin Windows desktop is the center of all you do on your computer, and it's a Spartan place (**FIGURE 13.3**).

FIGURE 13.3 There's not much to see on a fresh Windows desktop, but you can change all that.

In fact, on a brand new installation of Windows Vista, there are just three main elements on the desktop:

- The Recycle Bin, which is the equivalent of the trash on the Mac desktop.

- The taskbar, which includes the Start button and Notification Area (sometimes referred to as the System Tray). This is akin to the Dock and the menu bar on the Mac.

- The Sidebar, which contains gadgets that are similar to the widgets found in the Mac's Dashboard feature.

The Start button, which takes you to the Start menu, and the taskbar are at the heart of working with Windows. Let's take a look at them.

The Start Button

In versions of Windows prior to Vista, the Start button was actually labeled Start. But Microsoft got all artsy with its latest operating system, and the Start button is now just a blue globe with the Windows logo on it. Internally, Microsoft calls this the Pearl, but we'll stick with calling it the plain ol' Start button.

Click the Start button to get to the Start menu (**FIGURE 13.4**), which serves as a gateway to Windows' various components.

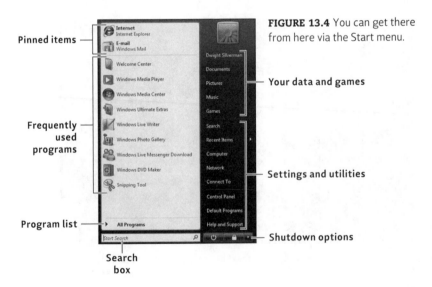

FIGURE 13.4 You can get there from here via the Start menu.

Pinned items

Frequently used programs

Program list

Search box

Your data and games

Settings and utilities

Shutdown options

The different areas of the Start menu provide access to programs and settings in a variety of ways:

- **Pinned items.** The programs icons that appear in the top left are said to be *pinned* to the Start menu. By default, Internet Explorer and Windows Mail appear here, but you can pin any program here by simply dragging its icon into this area.

- **Frequently used programs.** If you use a program often, it will appear in the middle-left part of the Start menu. The more often you launch a program, the higher it rises on the list. This list will change over time as you use programs.

- **Program list.** Click here to see a list of all the programs available to Windows. You can then click any one of them in the list to launch it.

- **Search box.** This is the equivalent of Spotlight on the Mac. And like Spotlight, Vista's search is very fast, and can even be used to launch a program simply by typing in its name and pressing Enter.

- **Your data and games**. At the top right of the Start menu are selections that take you to folders containing your important data: documents, photos, and music. There's also a link to Windows Vista's Games folder.

- **Settings and utilities**. The middle-right section features links to useful items and settings. Here you can access a more advanced search box, a list of recently opened documents, your computer's drives via Windows Explorer (which I'll detail later in this chapter), different network connections, the Control Panel (the Windows version of System Preferences), a list of default programs, and a Help and Support page.

- **Shutdown options.** These buttons give you a variety of ways of logging out of an account, putting your computer to sleep, hibernating the computer, locking the screen, switching to a different user, restarting, or powering down.

The Taskbar

The Windows taskbar is designed to give you quick access to running programs. It contains an area that gives you information about what some programs are doing, as well as provides quick access to features within some programs. It also has an area where you can park icons for programs you launch frequently.

In Figure 13.3, you can see the components of the taskbar. Here's a little more on what each does:

- **Taskbar main body.** The main body of the taskbar shows a button for each running program (**FIGURE 13.5**). If there are several instances of a program running, Windows may group them under one button, depending on how much room your taskbar has. You can minimize programs to the taskbar, and then restore them by clicking on their buttons. Or, if a program's window is hidden by others, you can bring it forward by clicking its Taskbar button.

FIGURE 13.5 Click a Taskbar button to bring a program forward, or see what's in a group of buttons, such as with Internet Explorer in this screenshot.

- **Quick Launch.** You can drag and drop icons into this area to the right of the Start button for easy access to frequently used programs.

- **Notification Area.** Here you'll find all kinds of information about your system. If you've got a notebook computer, for example, you'll see a battery meter. If you are connected to a wireless network, an icon here can tell you whether you're linked to the Internet. You can access Windows' volume meter from here. And other programs park icons here that give you access to their settings. You may see this referred to as the System Tray, its name from earlier versions of Windows.

You can tweak various parts of the taskbar, including where it appears on your screen. Want to put the taskbar at the top of your screen, so that it corresponds to the Mac's menu bar? Here's how:

1. Right-click an open area of the taskbar. A context menu appears, with the Lock the Taskbar option selected by default.

2. Deselect the Lock the Taskbar option. You'll know the taskbar is unlocked when a divider made of several dotted lines appears to the right of the Quick Launch area.

3. To move the taskbar to either the top, right, or left side of the screen, click and hold the taskbar and drag it into place, and then release.

4. To give the Quick Launch area room for more icons, click and hold on the divider and drag it to the right.

5. To re-lock the taskbar, right-click it and select Lock the Taskbar from the menu that appears.

Now that you understand the basics of how the taskbar and Start menu work, let's dive into Windows Explorer.

Exploring Windows Explorer

Even Mac users have heard of Internet Explorer, the browser that comes with Windows. It gets its name from Windows Explorer, the application that navigates Windows' drives and folders. It has been around since Windows 95, but got a major facelift in Windows Vista.

But before we explore the Explorer, you may want to know a little bit about how Windows' file system works.

About Windows' Drives and Folders

Unlike the Mac, in which drives sit right out on the desktop, drives in Windows are accessed through Windows Explorer. The easiest way to get to them is through the Start menu:

1. Click the Start button. The Start menu appears.

2. Click the Computer selection in the Start menu's right pane to open Windows Explorer (**FIGURE 13.6**).

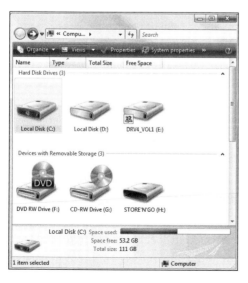

FIGURE 13.6 Windows' drives are accessed via Windows Explorer.

TIP

Want access to the C drive on your Windows desktop, in the same way that you have access to the Macintosh HD on the Mac desktop? In Computer view, left-click and hold the C drive icon and drag it onto the desktop. Windows will create a shortcut to the drive automatically. You can do this for any other folder as well, but a word of caution: If you use the left mouse button on most folders, you'll actually move the folder to the desktop, rather than just creating a shortcut. Instead, right-click and hold to drag, and when you release the icon, select Create Shortcut Here from the menu that appears.

The primary drive, on which the operating system and most programs are stored, is usually labeled as Drive C. Other drives get other letter designations: D, E, and so on. Drives A and B are reserved for floppy drives (remember them?).

The Computer view also shows all removable-storage drives, such as CD and DVD drives; external drives; and flash-memory-based devices, such thumb drives and memory card readers. Each one will also have a letter designation.

Double-clicking any of these drives shows you the files and folders stored on them, just as in the Mac.

Windows Vista's folders hold both the programs and the data they create. Your documents, photos, movies, music, and other data files are stored in your User folder, which is similar to the Home folder in the Mac. To get to your User folder:

1. Click the Start button, and the Start menu appears.

2. Click your name as it appears on the top right pane of the Start menu. Your User folder appears.

From here you'll see other folders labeled Documents, Music, Pictures, Videos, and more. This folder is your starting point for working with your data in Windows.

Now that you understand the structure of Windows' file system, let's learn more about Windows Explorer itself.

Inside Windows Explorer

Windows Explorer's windows look a lot like Mac's Finder windows (**FIGURE 13.7**).

Let's take a look at the window's components:

- **Back and forward buttons.** Just as with a browser viewing Web pages, you can move back and forth between folders you've visited by clicking these buttons.

- **Address bar.** This shows you where you are in Windows' file system. You can click any of the segments in the address path to go directly to that folder.

- **Search the folder.** Looking for a specific document within this folder? Enter a keyword to search on name, tags, or even content in documents within the current folder.

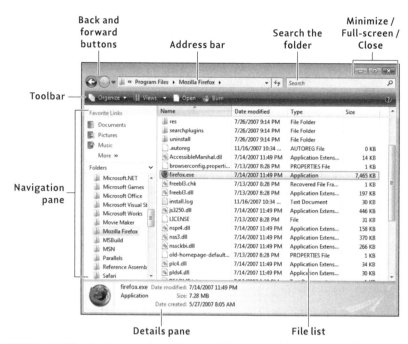

FIGURE 13.7 The Explorer window will remind Mac users of the Finder window.

- **Minimize/Full-screen/Close.** On Macintosh Finder windows, the equivalents for these buttons are on the top left. From left to right, the first button minimizes to the taskbar; the middle button will either make the window full-screen or restore it to its previous size, depending on its current state; the last button will close the window.

- **Toolbar.** The toolbar lets you change the look of the folder and work with files, such as burning them to a CD. What appears here depends on what's in the folder you're viewing. For example, in a folder with Word documents, e-mail is an option, allowing you to quickly send a file to a recipient.

- **Navigation pane.** Similar to the sidebar in Mac's Finder window, this pane gives you access to folders on your PC, as well as those of any computers on your network.

- **File list.** The center of the window, the file list displays your files and folders. You can change the look of files and folders by clicking the Views button in the toolbar (Figure 13.7) and having them display as icons instead of in a list, and you can even control the size of the icons.

- **Details pane.** Here you can see the details about any file you select in the file list. If it's a document, a photo, or a media file, you can change some of the file's attributes (such as the author's name), add a tag, or rate its content. Using Vista's advanced search, you can then search on the date you added for the file.

These are the folder components available by default, but there's one more part that makes the Explorer windows even more useful. The Preview pane lets you see an expanded view of a file without actually launching it. It's similar to Cover Flow view in Leopard's Finder.

To turn on the Preview pane:

1. In the folder in which you'd like to add a Preview pane, click the Organize button in the toolbar. A dropdown menu appears.

2. Hover your mouse cursor over the Layout item, and a secondary menu appears.

3. Select Preview Pane. The Preview pane opens on the right side of the Explorer window (**FIGURE 13.8**).

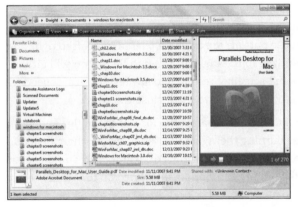

FIGURE 13.8
The Preview pane lets you see many types of files without having to open them.

4. Click a file to see it displayed in the Preview pane.

This is one of Vista's most useful features. It can display all kinds of files in their entirety. You can read complete Word or PDF files. And when you preview a video or music file, you can also watch or listen to them in a player that appears in the Preview screen.

Now that you understand the basics of how Windows works, let's look at some more advanced features of Microsoft's operating system.

chapter 14

Advanced Windows

Windows Vista is a big, sprawling, complex operating system. You can get by just fine by skimming its surface, just like you can with a Mac, but Windows has even more nooks and crannies.

And if you're running Windows on the Mac, there are several advanced aspects that are crucial to understand. They include getting your Windows system onto the Internet and creating a home network; installing and removing programs; updating Windows; and most importantly, protecting yourself against malicious programs like viruses, spyware, worms, and Trojans.

This chapter introduces you to just a few of the advanced features of Windows; it's by no means the complete picture. For that, I'll refer you to my first book, co-written with veteran author Larry Magid, *Microsoft Windows Vista: Peachpit Learning Series*.

Getting Online

How you connect to the Internet when running Windows on your Mac depends on a couple of factors: what type of network adapter your computer is using (wired or wireless), and whether you're running Windows virtually (Parallels Desktop or VMware Fusion) or natively (Boot Camp).

The simplest scenario involves using a hardwired Ethernet connection. In this case, it's just a matter of connecting the Ethernet cable to the Ethernet port on your Mac. Windows should connect automatically, regardless of whether you're running virtually or natively.

If you're connecting via Wi-Fi and running Windows natively, you'll need to pick a wireless network in a process that's similar to that used for the Mac, and which I'll detail later.

If you're using Wi-Fi and running Windows virtually, the process is similar to connecting via Ethernet. This is because both Parallels and Fusion piggyback on your Mac's network adapter. They don't care whether it's Ethernet or Wi-Fi—they just see an Internet connection is available.

Choosing Your Location

Whenever you establish a new network connection, Windows has a feature called Set Network Location that lets you decide what kind of security to provide. This allows you to be more open when you're connecting to a home network, but if you're on a notebook and connecting to, say, a public Wi-Fi hotspot, you can choose a setting with tighter security.

For this exercise, I presume you're connecting via Ethernet natively, or using either Ethernet or Wi-Fi virtually. Later I'll show you how to make a Wi-Fi connection using a native Windows installation.

1. Connect an Ethernet cable to your computer. Vista establishes a connection to the network, and the Set Network Location window appears (**FIGURE 14.1**).

FIGURE 14.1 Windows Vista provides different security settings based on where you are when you connect to the Internet.

2. Choose one of the following:

- **Home** or **Work.** Functionally, there's not much difference between Home and Work locations. Both allow you to see other computers on the network, and if you allow it, those computers can see yours.

- **Public Location.** This option hides the presence of your computer from others on a network. Use it when you're connected away from home, in hotels, coffee shops, libraries, and airports.

   If a User Account Control prompt appears, click Continue. The Successfully Set Network Settings window appears.

3. Click Close.

Once you have chosen a network location, you shouldn't have to go through this process again, unless you connect to a different network.

Connecting with Wi-Fi

If you're running Windows natively via Leopard's Boot Camp, then getting onto a Wi-Fi network involves using Vista's wireless connection process. It's similar to that used by the Mac.

To connect wirelessly via a native Windows setup:

1. With Windows powered up, make sure that you're in a location that has a wireless connection to the Internet.

2. Click the connection icon 🖳 in the taskbar's Notification Area to display the Not Connected menu.

3. Select Wireless Networks Are Available. A dialog box displaying a list of available networks appears (**FIGURE 14.2**).

FIGURE 14.2 Choose from both secure and unsecure connections from Vista's list of available Wi-Fi networks.

The networks will be labeled Security-Enabled or Unsecured. Access to the former requires some kind of passphrase or a letter–number combination string that you'll have to get from the network's operator. The passphrase is used to encrypt or scramble the signal, making it more secure. Access to the latter type of network is usually found in public places and won't require a passphrase. This type of network is convenient but not as secure.

The strength of the signal is indicated by the number of green bars shown in its listing.

4. For the purposes of this exercise, select the unsecured network with the best signal, and then click Connect. A warning box appears, saying that the network is unsecured.

5. Click Connect Anyway.

A window showing the progress of the connection appears, followed by a Successfully Connected window.

6. If you think you may visit this Wi-Fi hotspot regularly, check the Save This Network check box.

The next time you are within range of this hotspot, Vista will connect to it automatically as a preferred network.

7. Click Close. The Set Network Location window, shown in Figure 14.1, appears.

8. Choose Public Location. The Successfully Set Network Settings dialog box appears.

9. Click Close.

You're now connected wirelessly.

Managing Windows Programs

Once you're online, you can download and install thousands of Windows programs. And yes, you can also buy physical copies on CD or DVD. Sure, there are plenty of programs for the Mac, but the Windows software universe is far more expansive, given the larger installed base of Microsoft's operating system.

On one level, installing software on Windows is actually a little more straightforward than on the Mac. As I mentioned in Chapter 10, there are two different ways to install Mac software, depending on the program: either drag the executable into the Applications folder, or run an installer program. In Windows, nearly all software uses an installer.

Downloading and Installing Via the Web

To download and install a program from the Web (presuming you're using Internet Explorer 7 as your Web browser):

1. Click the link for the program you want to install. Vista presents a dialog box asking whether you want to run or save the file.

If you select Run, the installer is downloaded to a temporary folder on your computer, and then launched automatically. Select Save, and the file is saved to a location first so that you can launch it when you're ready. Because the latter option gives you a safety net by putting a copy of the file on your hard drive, it's often best to take that route.

2. Click Save. The Save As dialog box appears.

By default, Vista saves downloaded files to a Downloads folder within your user folder. If you'd like to store it somewhere else, click the Browse Folders button at the bottom of the dialog box. The Save As dialog box expands to provide you more choices (**FIGURE 14.3**). From here, you can navigate to almost any folder on your hard drive.

 **WARNING**

Not all Windows software is friendly. If you decide to download a program from an unfamiliar Web site, search on its name in your favorite search engine. If it's malware, you'll likely see others complaining about it. And never, ever download software that's touted via an unsolicited Web popup or spam e-mail. I'll discuss this more later in this chapter.

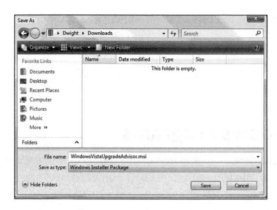

FIGURE 14.3 The Save As dialog lets you save a downloaded file to any location on your Windows hard drive.

3. Navigate to the location where you'd like to store the file.

4. Click Save.

5. Using Windows Explorer, locate the folder where you just stored the installer, and double-click its icon to start the installation process. If you stored it on the desktop, you can simply double-click it from there.

   You may see one of several different types of dialog boxes that want to confirm whether you really want to install this software; they will vary depending on the type of software you're installing. This is one of Vista's security features, User Account Control, designed to prevent malicious software from installing automatically.

6. Click Yes, OK, or Continue, depending on the dialog box, to confirm that you want to install the software. The installer launches.

7. Follow the prompts given by the installer, which will vary depending on the program you're installing, to complete the process.

You can find an icon for your newly installed software in the Programs list on the Start menu. Or the installer may have dropped an icon on the desktop or the Quick Launch bar.

Installing from a CD or DVD

Windows has a feature called AutoPlay that launches when a CD or DVD is inserted into an optical drive. It displays a box and asks if you want to run the program installed on it. This makes it fairly easy to launch an installer.

NOTE

The icons you find in the Programs list, the desktop, and the Quick Launch bar are not the software's executable files themselves. Unlike the Mac, Windows stores installed programs in separate system folders, and puts pointer icons called Shortcuts in easy-to-access locations. Note that if you delete one of these shortcuts—recognizable by the curved arrow in the lower left corner—you won't delete the program itself, just the shortcut. They are similar to aliases in the Mac.

To install software from a disc:

1. Insert the installation disc into your Mac's CD or DVD drive.

   If AutoPlay is enabled, the AutoPlay dialog box appears (**FIGURE 14.4**).

FIGURE 14.4 AutoPlay lets you launch an installer automatically after you insert a CD or DVD.

2. Do one of the following:

   ■ Click the option below Install or Run Program to start the installer.

   ■ Click Open Folder to View Files to be taken to the folder that contains the installer. (Do this if you want to look for read-me files or other instructions before installing the software.)

   ■ Select the option Always Do This for Software and Games if you don't want to see this dialog box again.

   Any of several types of User Account Control dialog boxes may appear.

3. Click Yes, OK, or Continue, depending on the prompt, to proceed with the installation.

4. Follow the installer's prompts to finish installing the software.

5. When the installation is done, press the Mac's CD/DVD Eject button to eject the disc.

Uninstalling Programs

When Windows programs are installed, crucial files for the software may be scattered in various folders across your hard drive. That's why it's important never to try to delete a Windows program simply by dragging its program folder to the Recycle Bin. Instead, you'll want to uninstall it.

Properly written Windows programs place an entry in a Control Panel module called Programs and Features. (In Windows XP and other older versions of Windows, the module is called Add/Remove Programs.) You'll want to use that to remove software you no longer plan to use.

To remove a program from Windows:

1. Click the Start button, and then select Control Panel from the right side of the Start menu. The Control Panel opens.

2. From the Program category, select Uninstall a Program. The Programs and Features window appears (**FIGURE 14.5**).

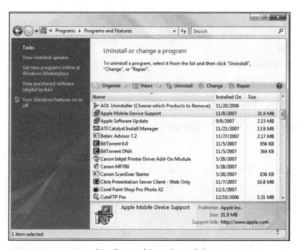

FIGURE 14.5 Use this Control Panel module to remove Windows programs.

3. Select an item from the list of installed programs, then click the Uninstall button in the toolbar. A User Account Control prompt appears.

4. Click Continue. The uninstall routine itself will present another prompt, asking whether you want to continue.

5. Click Yes or OK, depending on how the prompt is worded. A dialog box will show the progress, and will then indicate the process is complete.

6. Click OK to close the dialog box.

In some rare cases, a program may not have an entry in Programs and Features, but may still include an uninstaller. Usually, it's stored in the software's folder in the Program Files folder. To find it:

1. Click Start, and from the menu that displays, select Computer.

2. Double-click the C drive icon (or the icon for the drive where the program is stored). Windows Explorer opens.

3. Double-click the Program Files folder. You'll see a list of folders that contain programs.

4. Find the folder for the program you want to install and double-click it. Look for a file with a name such as Uninstall, Remove, or Unwise.

5. Double-click the uninstaller to begin the process, and follow its prompts.

Avoiding Malware

If you are a Macintosh user new to running Windows, this is probably the most important section in this book. Wisely or not, Mac users generally don't think about protecting themselves against viruses, spyware, worms, and Trojans. But if you are running Windows—and particularly if you are using it to connect to the Internet—it's something you need to think about . . . *a lot.*

In the "Staying Secure" section of Chapter 11, I talked about how the bad guys who write malicious software are motivated these days by greed. Their goal is often to take control of your Windows computer and turn into a spam-spewing machine. This can happen without your even knowing about it. Computers that have been appropriated in this way are called zombie PCs. Trust me, you don't want your computer to become a zombie.

In preparation for writing this book, I asked several Macintosh owners what they'd most want to know about running Windows, and each one mentioned the issue of malware. Because they run Macs, they said, they wouldn't even know what it looks like.

Recognizing Malware

Spyware, viruses, Trojans, and worms can get onto your computer in a variety of ways:

- **E-mail.** Some malware comes as an e-mail attachment, or through a link in the body of the mail. The attachment may itself be an executable file that installs malware on your computer, or it may be a Web page that takes you a site that attempts to install it. A link in an e-mail could take you directly to an malicious site.

- **Web pages.** If your computer is not up-to-date with patches for security vulnerability, a malicious Web page may try to exploit that flaw by using it to install malware. This is known as a "drive-by download," and it could happen without your even knowing about it.

- **Web popups.** One of the most common and most effective ways of planting malware on a user's computer is through a popup advertising software designed to block or remove malware. But the software you download and install as a result is actually just the opposite—a malware program.

- **Free software.** Not all software offered as free includes malware, but much of it is. Big-name commercial software, such as Microsoft Office or Adobe Photoshop, offered in "cracked" versions may contain malware. These are often offered through so-called "warez" sites.

- **Software crackers.** You may see programs that offer to crack the copy protection on commercial software. These may contain malware.

- **Browser plug-ins.** You may find sites that want you to install obscure plug-ins or what are called codecs to view certain kinds of video. If they're not among the common ones like Flash, Windows Media, RealMedia, or Silverlight, avoid them. You're most apt to find them on sites that offer unsavory content, such as pornography or gambling.

Notice something common to all these types of attacks? The user is the common thread: You have to do something that starts the process, whether it's downloading and installing something or going to a site that contains malicious software. Almost all forms of malware rely on what's known as "social engineering"—tricking you into doing something that installs the malware on your computer.

Preventing Malware

There are some basic steps you can take to keep malware from infecting your system. Most of them are common sense, but you'd be surprised how many people don't take these steps and fall prey to malicious software.

- **Don't go where you shouldn't.** As I mentioned, sites that feature questionable content are most apt to attempt to deliver malware on your computer. The best advice I can give you is: Live clean, and your Windows installation will stay clean. Avoid porn, gambling, illegal software, free music, and movie sites. If it feels the least bit funny going there, then don't go there.

- **Be wary of attachments and e-mail links.** Just because you receive an e-mail from someone you trust doesn't mean that e-mail is trustworthy. Modern malware that's distributed via e-mail can forge or spoof the From address, making it appear to come from someone else. A good rule of thumb: If you weren't expecting an e-mail with an attachment from someone, don't launch that attachment. It's even smart not to click random links that appear to be sent from someone you know. You can always reply and ask the sender if they did indeed send the suspicious e-mail.

- **Install and use antivirus and antispyware programs.** Although many Mac users don't run antivirus software, it's a must if you're using Windows. Vista comes with an excellent antispyware program, Windows Defender, but it does not have an antivirus component. You've probably heard of Norton Antivirus (www.symantec.com) and McAfee VirusScan (www.mcafee.com). But there are plenty of others, including the free AVG Free (free.grisoft.com) and the well-reviewed NOD32 (www.eset.com). Check the reviews of antivirus products at reputable tech sites such as www.pcmag.com and www.pcworld.com

- **Don't buy unsolicited software.** Never, ever buy software that's touted via a Web popup, or from an unsolicited e-mail or spam. Web popups will often warn you that you have a virus, and you must have a specific program to remove it. Spam will try to sell you brand-name products at ridiculously low prices. Avoid these; often they are programs that actually install malware on your machine.

Removing Malware

If you do get a malware infection, many of the programs designed to prevent its installation can also remove it. But malware can be tricky to remove, and some programs are better than others.

Two good programs to have in your arsenal are SpyBot Search and Destroy (www.safer-networking.org) and AdAware (www.lavasoftusa.com). Both are free, and if Windows Defender or another anti-malware program doesn't work, you can try those.

I've also written a series for the *Houston Chronicle* about removing malware. You can follow my step-by-step instructions at www.chron.com/spyware.

But some malware is so tenacious that the only way to get rid of it is to wipe your Windows hard drive clean and reinstall the operating system. This is where running Windows virtually, in Parallels Desktop or VMware Fusion, comes in handy.

As I mentioned in Chapter 5 for Parallels and Chapter 8 for Fusion, you can take snapshots of your Windows installation's state and restore it if you get infected. Or, you can restore your virtual machine from a copy or a backup of it. This is much easier than formatting your Boot Camp partition and reinstalling Windows from scratch.

Can a Windows Virus Affect the Mac?

One of the more common questions I hear from Mac users who want to run Windows is whether a malware infection in their Windows installation will have an effect on the Macintosh side.

The general answer is no. At this writing, there are no cross-platform malware programs that can leap across the Windows and Mac operating systems. However, that doesn't mean such a program will never be written.

It's theoretically possible for a Windows or a Mac virus to do something to the structure of a Mac hard drive, damaging both operating systems. But it would have to leap many security barriers to do so, and would likely involve social engineering that would require a user to install something in an unusual way.

This is another reason why Macintosh users should install and use anti-malware software on the Mac, as well as on Windows. You never know what threats will appear in the future.

Keeping Windows Updated

One of your best protections against malware is to keep Windows updated with all its latest patches and fixes. Microsoft automates this process with a feature called Windows Update, which automatically downloads fixes and alerts you to their presence. If you leave your computer on overnight, by default Windows will automatically install them at 3 a.m. after they've been received.

Apple dispatches its updates on an as-needed basis, but Microsoft waits until the second Tuesday of every month, which techies refer to as Patch Tuesday. Microsoft does this because many of its corporate customers want a regular schedule of updates. This allows businesses to test patches before applying them to potentially thousands of machines.

Manually updating Windows

When new patches are available, you'll see the Windows Update icon in the Notification Area. You can wait until 3 a.m. and let Windows install them, or you can do it yourself.

1. When you see the Windows Update icon in the Notification Area, click it. The Windows Update window opens (**FIGURE 14.6**).

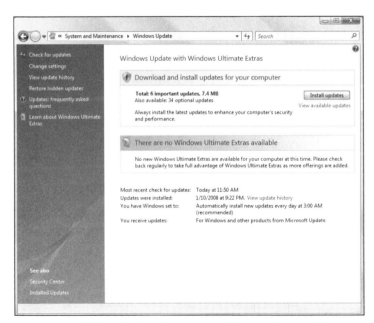

FIGURE 14.6 Windows Update lets you control how patches and fixes are delivered to your computer.

2. Click Install Updates.

   The window will minimize back to the Notification Area, while the updates are installed. When it's complete, a new window appears.

3. If a reboot is required to complete the installation, you'll be prompted to restart. Click Restart, and your computer will reboot.

4. If no reboot is required, you'll be told the updates are installed. Click Finish to close the window.

Changing how Windows updates

It's best to leave Windows Update's default settings alone, but if you want to change them, here's how:

1. Click Start, Control Panel, and then System and Maintenance. The System and Maintenance module appears.

2. Select Windows Update. The Windows Update window appears.

3. Click Change Settings in the left pane. The Change Setting window appears (**FIGURE 14.7**).

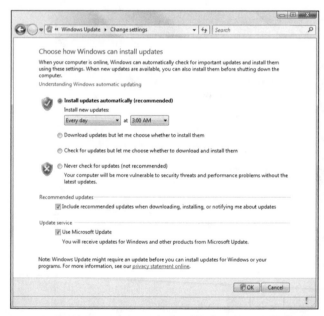

FIGURE 14.7 You can change whether Windows automatically updates your computer here. But it's best to leave the default settings in place.

As mentioned earlier, the default is to install updates at 3 a.m. after they are received.

You have several choices for changing them.

4. To change the frequency or time of day, click one of the two drop-down menus under Install New Updates.

5. To download the patches but install them manually, select "Download updates but let me choose whether to install them."

6. To simply have Windows alert you that patches are available, but not download them, select "Check for updates but let me choose whether to download and install them."

7. If you want no automated update services—and this is *not* recommended—select "Never check for updates."

8. Click OK when you're finished, and click Continue to clear the User Account Control prompt.

What About Updating Drivers?

One the nicest things about running Windows on your Mac is that, for the most part, you don't have to worry about hardware driver updates. Whether you're running Windows virtually or natively, updating drivers is taken care of for you.

If you've installed Windows using Apple's Boot Camp, new drivers are delivered via Apple's Software Update program. You'll be alerted when new drivers are available; just follow the prompts to download and install them.

And both Parallels Desktop for Mac and VMware Fusion update Windows drivers via their respective Tools features (Parallels Tools and VMware Tools). When new versions of the Tools programs are available, Parallels or Fusion alerts you.

Staying Secure

Windows Vista is Microsoft's most secure operating system. It has multiple features designed to create layers of security, which make it more difficult for hackers to get into your system, or for malware to be installed.

Vista includes a central location where all its security features are maintained. The Security Center, found in the Control Panel, lets you manage the Windows Firewall, your spyware and antispyware programs, automatic updates, and User Account Control.

To access the Security Center and see all that it can control:

1. Click Start, and then Control Panel. The Control Panel appears.

2. Under the Security heading, select Check This Computer's Security Status. The Windows Security Center opens (**FIGURE 14.8**).

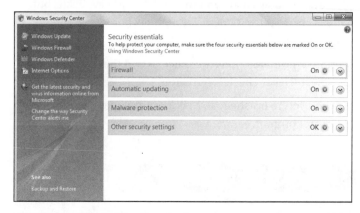

FIGURE 14.8 The Windows Security Center lets you see the status of key security features at a glance.

You'll see four categories: Firewall, Automatic Updating, Malware Protection, and Other Security Settings. If all is well, each category will be flagged with the word On and a green light. If there are problems, the category header will turn yellow or red, with a description of the problem below it (**FIGURE 14.9**).

FIGURE 14.9 When something's not right, the category header will warn you with a color change and details about the issue.

If you want, you can see a lot more information about these categories.

3. Click the down arrow on the right side of each category. More information appears about each one.

4. To change the settings for Windows Update, Window Firewall, or Windows Defender, select the items for them in the upper left pane of the Security Center. Individual control panels will open for each one.

5. When you are done making changes, close the control panels, and then close the Security Center.

Again, it's generally best to leave Windows' security default settings as they are. That will ensure Windows stays running smoothly and safely on your Mac.

index